Being Is The New Doing

Being Is the New Doing

A Divine Guide to Owning Your Energy, Time, and Peace of Mind

Radiah Rhodes

Being is the New Doing
A Divine Guide to Owning your Energy, Time, and Peace of Mind

Copyright © 2018 Radiah Rhodes
Published by Evok Life by Design Books

Cover by Ekiuwa Evbuomwan

Cover Photo Credit: Lydia Kearney Carlis, PhD

Paperback ISBN: 978-1983580963

Library of Congress Control Number: 2017959275

First Print Edition January 2018

DEDICATION

To my exceptional husband, Calvin, who sets the vision and leads with love, passion, and laughter. To my kind and brilliant children, Sydney and Brayden, who shine brighter than a thousand suns. Thank you for giving me the inspiration and space to create this work and write this book. I hope you're as proud of me as I am of you.

Thank you to my mother, Patty, for showing me the strength and freedom to *be* myself under any circumstances. Here's to my father, Alan, for music, art, books, and the First Day of May. Thank you for asking me, "Who are you?" and sparking a movement.

To my phenomenal partner, Dr. Roni, for being willing and committed to "help her girl out" and my boss partner, Tawana, for demonstrating authentic power unlike anyone I had ever seen. Thank you for "touching and agreeing" on a vision of what is possible, and to the many BEprinters™ who trusted us enough to invite Evók on their journey.

I say thank you, I love you, I got you, and I am you.
Namaste.

CONTENTS

ACKNOWLEDGMENTS

I have the fullest heart, and I am deeply grateful for my grandparents, Aubrey and Clara Burgess, Ellis and Nettie Goode, and Samuel and Erika Barnes. Every day of my life has been shaped by your love and care.

To Juanita for loving me like your own daughter and sharing your light in some of my darkest and brightest moments. To Freddie Steverson who provided for my mother and me during some of the toughest times, thank you. To my mother-in-law, Della, your love and kindness are your superpowers that lift our family higher. To my brothers Darris and Damion, where (and who) would I be without your love and protection? Thank you to my aunties and uncles, who pray for me and love on me constantly. Special love and thanks to my uncle AC, a.k.a. "the People's Uncle," for keeping me healthy and well fed. To my Uncle Lonnie who keeps me smiling and laughing, and my Uncle Jimmy for your constant prayers and love. A huge shout-out to all of my cousins, Tara, Jena, Garrett, Dhia, Cleo, Todd, Pierre, Jackie, Leafus, Raymond, and all my Baskerville cousins—I love y'all to life! To my nieces and nephews, I love you and pray for your health, happiness, and success daily. Sahmir Mahdi, I am so proud of you.

Thank you to the Johnson, Henson, Harrell, and Malone families for taking care of me and being a comfort in the middle of chaos. Joy, Erica, Stacey, and Tiffany, you're the best sisters I could ever pray for. I love you.

Wendy Blue, Dr. Stephanie Adams, and Jewel Best, I literally "never would have made it without you." You believed in me when I had no clue. You invested in me spiritually, emotionally, and financially and we made it through. Thank You!

To the Real Coach Shawn, thank you for reintroducing me to tennis and for reminding me that I'm "designed to win". I am so grateful for Dr. Njide Udochi, who was the ultimate guardian of my physical and mental health. Thank you for your regular doses of tough love and compassion and for seeing me through to full restoration.

A huge thank you to Dr. Larthenia Howard for midwifing this book into the world. To Kristen Evans, Tracy G., and Maximillion Pick for helping me find my voice in a sea of noise and a mix of guru, engineer, and Jersey girl.

To my squad of badass women: Leslie Gordon, Dr. Measha Peterson, Dana Harvey, Nina Payne, Dr. Jeri Dyson, Tasha Brown, Luchana Sumpter, Stephanie Avinger, Nichole Wormsley, Sylvia Alston, Melanie Davis, Stacey Pinkett, Jamarra Mitchell, Dara Overstreet, Veronica Very, Annie Vonheim, Jen Sevilla, Candace McLaren, Janeen Uzzell, Juliet Gilliam, Nneka Rimmer, Roslyn Ashford, Chaun Bunt, Ricki Fairley, Adriane Keepler, Dr. Rachel Talton, Lynn Selby, Dr. Lydia Kearney Carlis, Dr. Stacey Eadie, and Dr. Michelle Reed. Thank you for role modeling, motivating, and challenging me to be better and fly higher. #BGM

PREFACE

I am a seeker and a sufferer. I have both high moments of enthusiastic optimism and low moments of deep pain and mourning. I was born a Pisces, one fish upstream and one downstream. The day I came home, a newborn, my grandfather drove me from the hospital to our housing projects, in a limousine. March 11, 1975—a time of great contrast where youth protested hard and partied harder. There was a revolution, free love, war, and drugs, and I was born smack in the middle of that time. Both nature and nurture. I am naturally a child of duality and a product of what my circumstances molded me to become.

For as long as I can remember, I had questions. I wanted to

know more and do more. I would sit in the middle of my grandmother's living room floor and read through her atlas and encyclopedias to feed my mind. My father's brother, Uncle Jimmy, was a student under Alvin Ailey and Judith Jamison in New York. He was an accomplished dancer and taught me everything he knew, from ballet to violin to foreign languages. My imagination ran wild, and I spent hours synthesizing all this new information. I loved learning, and my intelligence became my way to order the chaos that filled the background of my life.

Being born in New Jersey to a single black mother of three with no money and little support brought plenty of hard times. My mother was raised by her grandparents in those same housing projects and became a teenage wife and mother of two boys before she began dating my father and created me. My brothers and I thought our mother was the strongest, smartest, and most beautiful woman we had ever seen. With her head held high and no apologies, Mommy worked hard and did the best with what she had to take care of us. It was a constant struggle; we were often left alone or with neighbors, and there were many times we had no food. My mother had to endure the consequences of some tough decisions, specifically having to see her children live with family and friends when she struggled to make ends meet.

We all started out living together with my father's parents in a pretty stable household. My grandfather, Pop Pop, had his regular job as a limousine driver for a popular musician at the time, and Nanny was a registered nurse who worked the graveyard shift for as long as I can remember. My grandparents loved me beyond life, and because of them I knew what it felt like to be deeply cared for and loved just because I existed.

After a short time we moved from staying with my grandparents, beginning a back and forth pattern of living between their home and several apartments with and without my father. By the time I was three-years old, my parents' relationship was over. My brothers had gone to live with their father's family, and my mother and I were on our own. As a daddy's girl, I was traumatized every time my father left or dropped me off from a visit. It was during this time my father started dating a woman who would later become my stepmother, exposing my father and me to a whole new standard of living.

Juanita came from a military family with both parents and three siblings raised in the beautiful home where we spent most of our time. Those times provided me with warmth, culture, and all types of luxuries I had never seen before. There was fine art, gourmet foods, dinner parties with extended family and friends, pressed linens, polished silver, crystal glasses, and a host of experiences that I know have inspired my passion for beauty and a high quality lifestyle to this day.

I would go back and forth living in environments that could not have been more different. My childhood was spent going from the close-knit housing projects with Pop Pop and Nanny one week, to being alone in an apartment hungry for food the next, to spending my weekends in a four-bedroom home filled with delicacies and cultural details I couldn't even pronounce. I lived in about ten different homes (including living with other family members and friends) until I graduated from high school. Going from place to place was like night and day, and there was always a void. I was either missing my mother or father, lacking the safety and care of being with Pop Pop and Nanny, or anticipating new experiences at Grandma and Grandpa's. Stability came in pockets but was always interrupted by a whole world of drug dealing, drug addiction, alcoholism, and depression playing out in the background. What I did see led to some despairing moments, and through nothing but grace, there was a great deal I didn't see.

I'm sharing this for two main reasons. One, I was raised in a highly unstable environment where painful experiences cultivated in me an attachment to stability and a fear of abandonment that has run a large part of my life. The attachment was so strong it created a pattern of suffering that has been one of my toughest challenges to break. Two, as unstable as my childhood was, it was my normal, and the exposure to both the rough, dark experiences and the rich and light experiences formed my foundational beliefs; no matter how dark it gets, there is always light. There is always a way up, out, and through, and all things work together for my good.

So as a child of duality, I developed a sufferer's heart with a seeker's mind. I have an amazing ability to shift from one space to another expanding and transforming myself in the process. Resilience, agility, creativity, and problem-solving are my superpowers. My seeking attracted the attention of people in my community who cared, and grace started pouring into my life. School was an escape that gave me a place to use my intellect. I stood out academically, and my teachers took notice.

In third grade I was sent to a gifted and talented program. I attended a magnet school in Philadelphia during middle school, and as a high school sophomore I was accepted into a summer program at Stevens Institute of Technology where I discovered engineering. I garnered top honors in high school and went on to graduate from North Carolina State University with a bachelor's of science degree in engineering. I kept it moving and achieved a position of importance and influence with one of the most prominent companies in the world. I married my college sweetheart, Calvin, and in less than two years we had two adorable children, built a beautiful home, and launched a successful IT firm.

Forget Wonder Woman. I was Wonder Woman, Superwoman, and Batgirl all combined. I started from chaos and through a sound mind, hard work, faith, and grace, I built a life worthy of dreams. I had escaped my childhood and finally made it. I was not playing with life; I had created a life that was rock solid! It was not only stable on the outside, I even did the inside work. I prayed, meditated, worked out, read all the books, went to church and therapy. It was not a game, I was committed to building the stable life I never had and always wanted.

And yet something was still profoundly wrong. My seeking mind had not only given me the exterior world I always wanted, but I had "done the work" to heal on the inside as well. Still, with everything I was doing to live how I wanted, as life always does, it caught up with me.

My moment of reckoning came about two years into marriage when each night I would come home to my perfect house from my steady job, kiss my amazing husband, check on my thriving toddlers … and then crawl into the corner of my bedroom where I would curl up and cry.

For hours. Suffering.

Being a new wife to an entrepreneur focused on growing a business, having two children sixteen months apart (while commuting two hours daily to work ten-hour days) was too damn much. As accomplished and blessed as it all was, the level of significant change was overwhelming and triggered my fear-based pattern of instability. I was completely off center and burning out fast.

My husband couldn't rescue me from my overwhelm. I felt it was too much drama to share with friends, shit, I didn't even want to talk about it to myself. Therapy felt comforting, and church soothed my soul but neither offered practical, real-life solutions. What could I do? One night I ended up in an excel spreadsheet trying to fix my life, and my seeker's mind started charting out the problem. I'm an engineer, I can figure this out. It worked in my job. Why wouldn't it here?

So each night, there I was, desperately typing out my emotions to vent and order the chaos through my laptop. What was the pattern, where was the common thread? If I couldn't identify the problem how the hell was I supposed to create a solution? Here's what I uncovered.

DOING THE MOST

My suffering had sent me seeking, and I had become an overdoer with a tendency for going too hard and grinding to regain stability. This was the pattern. When instability shows up, I suffer, start to panic, my mind starts churning, and I start seeking, striving, and doing whatever I can to avoid and fight the pain of instability. Yes, I am a doer. In fact, doing was my badge of honor. Whenever there was a question, need, or problem, I knew what to do when to do it, and how to do it to get the problem answered or resolved. I spent twenty years in corporate America getting results by "doing," and as an engineer and project manager, I became a "master" executioner. In short, doing became my natural go-to for survival until doing stopped working and left me miserable, exhausted, and pissed.

The truth was simple—I wasn't happy. The problem was devastating. I had done everything I was supposed to do to be happy, and I was still miserable. Remember, I was healthy and relatively fit, I had a successful husband, two growing children, a solid career, both parents living, a nice home, yada yada yada, you name it: check, check, and check—it was all there. And I wasn't happy. Did I say I was miserable? And exhausted, and pissed with a side of guilt, and ironically, there was nothing I could do to fix it.

THE MAGIC QUESTION

One morning I was on my way into work dreading the commute, so I called my father. I was on the phone analyzing (aka complaining about) everything from corporate structures, to family dynamics, to who knows what else. I'm sure it was good because I have a way of making complaining sound like this objective, in control, intellectual evaluation of someone else's theoretical problem. Whatever I was saying, my dad heard me out. He let me say my piece, and then he stopped me. He asked me in a matter-of-fact tone, "Stretch …" (that's my nickname) "Who are you?"

Wait, what? I was stopped in my tracks. Trying to do something to answer the question, I immediately responded with a bunch of other questions: "What do you mean? How do you want me to answer that? Can you give me an example?"

He said, "No. Take some time with that question, and call me back when you have an answer."

I realized that as much as I had thought about what and how I wanted to be, what I wanted to accomplish, or why I wanted it, I had never stopped and taken the time to deliberately think about who I was.

It took me about a week. I went back to my bedroom corner

and through more prayers, tears, and typing ... I got it!

I called him and said, "Daddy, I know who I am, " and he said, "Okay, who are you?"

I said, "I am Life-Changing Love!"

His response was, "Yes, you are, and yes, you got it!" Life-Changing Love was my declaration, and with his affirmation, it was the very beginning of a whole new life for me.

I had never thoughtfully asked myself this question. I spent years suffering, seeking, striving, and achieving without knowing who was driving all of it. My why was simple, clear, and compelling, I wanted a stable life to free me from my past pain. But who's why was it? Having a why without clarity of my who had me unconsciously running from a past of suffering believing it would be fixed by a future of accomplishments. When that didn't work, I got stuck and the simple question, "Who are you?" set an answer in motion that changed everything.

Who you are sets the entire context for what matters to you, and why. What you do and why you do it occurs inside of the context of the beliefs, thoughts, and emotional patterns of who you are. As a high performing doer, I didn't need much to stay busy and motivated. There were a thousand great reasons to do and accomplish so much. My why fueled my actions, but it was driven by my ego identity and fear. It got shit done and built a hell of a life by anyone's standards, but it also drove me out of alignment and down an unfulfilling path for myself. Declaring and defining who I was allowed me to shed my attachment to stability and open up to possibilities from a clear and aligned space of love, not fear. As Life-Changing Love, I was able to tap into the source of the who that was doing all the doing. Although it sounded broad and vague, I was at a point where the tangible and concrete parts of my life weren't adding up and what I knew for sure was that when I focused on love, life changed. I held onto that fact and rallied my whole being—my life—around that one answer.

And, as they say, that has made all the difference.

FUELED AND ON FIRE

As Life-Changing Love, the time spent on my bedroom floor turned my tears and typing into creative magic. I began to redesign myself, one truth at a time. I literally opened a new Excel spreadsheet and declared statement by statement who I was, who I wasn't, what I liked, what I was *not going to do*, and anything else I could think of that was true to me.

I thought about what I knew I was good at, what I loved, and what I dreamed about. I listed my standards for health, marriage, and money. I charted my goals and an action plan to make it real. I captured all of it, and before I knew it, I had documented a clear, definitive vision. I had a plan for my life, and had saved them all as tabs in an Excel file named "I Am."

Thank God for my engineering tendencies, because the practicality of that spreadsheet helped me wade through a sea of emotions without drowning. It literally kept me out of my feelings enough to move beyond the normal indulgent venting into pretty journals to strategizing an actual plan forward. Excel and PowerPoint were my BFFs, and I used the two to design a future and life I was inspired by.

I now had a why and a to-do list based on my passions, backed by purpose, and grounded in my truth. I had designed a powerful identity and anatomy of Who I was with no excuses, no confusion, and no limitations. I became highly intentional focusing on meaningful actions like investing my time, energy, and money into things that were aligned with who I was as Life-Changing Love. Things completely shifted. I stopped suffering and felt a sense of ease from not only knowing what to do but from being grounded and fully aligned with who I was. I felt free and on fire to embody the woman, wife, mother, and professional I had defined.

I was expanding and taking on things I had put off because I was tired or already doing too much. I had more energy than ever with even more responsibility. There was something new and different about this vision and plan that made it more real, effortless, and much more powerful. It was me. After three months, and about every three months after that, I found myself going back, updating my plan, and being in awe of the changes in my life.

LIFE TRANSFORMED

For three years I worked this process, quarter by quarter, and today it's the way I live. I tell people all the time: some things have changed and many have stayed the same. What's significant is that I enjoy it all immensely! No more misery. My life is so deeply good and fulfilling and the reality of constant change is no longer a threat.

I realized the power of starting with a clear answer to the question "who am I?" and moving with highly aligned, and conscious intentional action, is the most transformational way to create a meaningful life. To top that off, the blessing of my engineering mind has allowed me to design a process, of answering that one question in a way that is specific, potent, and repeatable. I call it BEprinting™.

I am writing this book to share a small yet hugely impactful piece of that process. My desire is that it serve as a straightshooting tool to help you break through the fog of confusion about who you are. Break out of the cycle of doing too much to have what you want, and break into the exact experience of life you desire.

Here's to intense passion, conscious intention, and Life-Changing Love.

Here's to the seekers. Here's to the life architects. Here's to the soul explorers.

Here's to you!

INTRODUCTION

You're a human being, not a human doing.
—Dr. Wayne Dyer, American Philosopher

YOU'RE DOING TOO MUCH

How is it that you can make all the *right* choices, do all the *right* things to the best of your ability, keep it all together and still find yourself on the wrong side of your own life? The simple answer is you're doing too much. More specifically, you're doing too much without knowing *who* is doing all the doing and why any of it matters to you.

You're jumping through hoops for everything and everyone. You're the one who goes above and beyond to the extra mile while wondering where you fit in. Time feels rushed, and you run on fumes saving everyone around you. But who is saving you? Life is still good; you feel grateful for your blessings and good fortune but who is it all for?

Where do you enter the equation of your own life? How do you own your life instead of doing so much to earn it? To be clear, action is absolutely necessary to make progress, but endless effort focused on things you have a small connection to does nothing but drain you and pull you out of alignment from the life you want. Living a life in alignment with who you are creates energy, builds momentum, and doesn't require back to back activity to create results.

Taking deliberate action from a place of personal truth, priority, passion, and purpose brings fulfillment, enjoyment, and peace of mind.

But how often do you take the time or energy to define your personal truth? When we have the time, we try to figure out what our passion or purpose is and often struggle with questioning whether it's this or that particular thing. We hope for that one magical cause that we believe will light us on fire. We believe if we're passionately energized it should change everything. So we look for signs and signals to tell us we've found it, secretly wanting it to *find* us and make it easier.

Some of us do take the time to get clear, but then get caught up in all the busy that goes on day to day, finding ourselves off-center and in need of a *major* recharge. Either way, we keep doing and end up moving further and further away from what matters. We feel frazzled, tired, and guilty for not being able to get it all done and missing what's important to us.

BEING IS THE NEW DOING

This book is about helping you recognize the position you're occupying in your life. It is a tool to reclaim your energy, time, and peace of mind by owning who you are and how you show up. Energy, time, and peace of mind are our three most valuable resources, yet we give them away so freely. Energy is our very life source, time is non-renewable, and how can you be present to experience life's gifts and pleasures without peace of mind? These resources are the core of a fulfilling, enjoyable, meaningful, and impactful life. *Being Is the New Doing* will help you master a method of reconnecting with who you are, owning your energy, and shifting out of the downward cycle of habitual and subconscious *doing* that drains your resources. You will move to a place where you take meaningful action from a deep knowledge of who you are and the core of who you define yourself to be. You'll learn to tap into your very own passions and purpose as the fuel for what you do and instead of feeling exhausted, guilty, or overwhelmed you feel peaceful, energized, and powerful.

Let me repeat this point: Doing is a must. Without question, doing is how we create the world around us. However, who is it that's doing all this doing? Is it the sleep deprived, prone to snap at any moment mom, or the relaxed and well-rested mom who's had her tea or coffee and some time to herself to meditate and breathe deeply in peace? Who you are being when you take action matters most. Who you are being dictates the type and intensity of energy you engage and therefore your experience and outcome as a result of that engagement.

Psychologist Abraham Maslow said, "If you only have a hammer, you tend to see every problem as a nail." If who you're being is a hammer in a given situation, then you'll repeatedly pound the things around you. In some cases, this may be effective, even necessary, but in other cases being a hammer would wreak havoc. How often are you aware of *who* you're being at a given moment? Rarely, right? That is how it was for me, walking around being who I thought I should be, reacting to whatever came up based on how I thought I should act. I lacked awareness of who I was being, and there was a disconnect between my world of doing and what I was experiencing in real life.

This lack of awareness is exactly how you end up being surprised when you look up and find yourself way to the left of your priorities or feeling blindsided by how the world responds to your actions. You'll find yourself saying, "That wasn't my intention," when someone gets upset or offended by something you said or did. It's also how we spend so much time, and effort racking up accomplishments and still feel a void or unfulfilled at the end of the day. This is the result when all of our *doing* is not consistent with our core *being* and the impact we want to have in a situation.

As a transformed *doer,* I have created and experienced

exceedingly and abundantly more fulfillment from being than I ever have by doing. It isn't always easy to make the shift from doing to being. Even now my tendencies to *just do it* come up. Sometimes I'm impatient, or straight-up arrogant, and don't feel like allowing or waiting for something to work itself out, even though it always does. It's not always easy to determine when to take action and when to press pause. It takes presence and clarity, high intention, even faith. It's not easy to cultivate these practices until they're second nature and readily available when the temptation to get busy doing comes up. It's not easy, but it's worth it.

Leading a busy life with a tight schedule, multiple demands, and critical deliverables make it easy to get caught up and consumed by activity. You start to focus on what you're doing and not doing, only to feel like something is still missing ... and you're right, something is missing because the results are one-sided. Focusing on doing without attention, and awareness of your being takes more time, taxes your energy, and causes a gap in how you feel once you get the tangible result.

You exhaust yourself to get the promotion but are completely turned off by the new job. You finally get engaged but still feel alone. You lose the weight but are constantly worried about gaining it all back again, depriving yourself of foods you enjoy. How do you stay aligned in a world that is constantly pulling you up, down, and off track from your true self?

Being Is the New Doing is a mind-set you can tap into to re-center and shift yourself back on track. Whether you're suffering or experiencing sovereignty, consciously shifting from one level of being to another can create the practice of living a meaningful life on your own terms. I know suffering doesn't sound good, it's not something most of us want to admit, but it happens. Suffering can sneak up on you. One moment you're passionate about something and the next you hit a brick wall and feel like you're stuck in the same cycle over and over again causing you to suffer. Then you remind yourself, life is still good, right? So you take a deep breath, move your energy up a few levels, and settle into a safe, comfortable space until something else changes and you shift again. Then on the other side, there's sovereignty. We don't often identify ourselves as having sovereignty over life. It's a concept that sounds grand and powerful but not attainable or sustainable given the amount of change surrounding us.

Being Is the New Doing will, one level at a time, shine a light on who you're being and walk you through how to identify, own, and shift your *level of being* to match and align with what you want. Each chapter will guide you through a specific level of intention, sharing stories from my life as a mirror for you to see yourself. My stories are ordinary stories that reflect existing truths, my personal experiences, and divine moments I download from time to time. For each level of intention I share ways of being that enable you to shift your consciousness and become present with your best and truest self. These ways of being can help you alleviate pain and hardship, release habits that no longer work for you, and restore alignment with your goals. They are common ways of being familiar to many of us, so as you read each chapter, you can connect to your own truth and see a pathway to owning your full potential and beyond. These levels of being are my personal go-to to transform my life, so I'll do my best to convey it in a way that helps you transform yours.

If you choose to go "all in" and learn the concepts and tools in this book,

- You will get clear and tell the truth about where you are in relationship and commitment to YOU and what matters most
- You will learn to free yourself up in moments and cycles that normally drain your energy without struggling and feeling guilty
- You will define who you are and align your time and energy accordingly
- You will reconnect to your passion and creativity as fuel for new beginnings and outcomes and
- You will significantly grow in your purpose and intention as you focus on what's important to you
- You no longer have to wait for a crisis to force you to change, you'll become skilled at a process to transform yourself whenever you choose and create the experiences you want under any circumstances.

If you're finally ready to break the busy cycle of doing and start being who you are designed to *be* … *let's go*!

PART I

THE MODEL

$$ARE^{BE+DO} = HAVE$$

$ARE^{BE+DO} = HAVE$ is the foundational model I use for creating goals and outcomes in real life. The concepts in the model set the basis and context for the tool and practices in this book. The model starts with who you ARE at the core of your existence and as energy here in this world. Then *who you ARE* is raised by the power of *who you're BEing* and *what you DO* to create *what you HAVE* as results, experiences, and impact. In short, who you *are* gets channeled through your *being* and *doing* to create the results and experiences you *have*. This equation is a tweak to an old model and opens up a new perspective on how you can own your energy and create what you want in a given situation. Like any equation, you can look at the results produced and trace it directly back to the components of that equation. The same idea works for you. With the model and tools in this section, you can connect the dots backward and most importantly forward to learn how to align who you are with who you're being and what you do to create exactly what you want to have in any moment.

CHAPTER 1

WHO ARE YOU?

We're made of star stuff; we are a way for the cosmos to know itself.
—Carl Sagan, American Astronomer

Let's start at the beginning with the profound question my father asked me that set all of this in motion.

Who are you?

Who you are is a creator. You are literally star stuff. A composite of the elements that make up the stars. Whether you believe in the science of your cosmic makeup or the spiritual truth of a higher power, you are infinite, and words cannot completely describe who you are. Words can only give you an idea of who you are because who you are is beyond words, concepts, and ideas. You are unlimited potential energy and if you don't believe that—

stop reading right here. Don't waste your time because that is the fundamental belief that governs every step we're going to take together. It's the belief that you are made of the same stuff as the stars and are intrinsically connected to that same life-giving power. It's spirit, it's science, it's reality, and it's powerful.

It took a while for me to see and absorb that truth. When my work environment was toxic, my relationship was a hot mess, and I was nursing two babies sixteen months apart, I felt trapped and nowhere near unlimited. My thoughts and emotions were either out of control or over-controlled, leaving me in mental chaos believing I was at my absolute limit. Acting from my tendency to start doing, I went to the bookstore and came across Joyce Meyer's *Battlefield of the Mind*, which was exactly what I needed to get myself together. As an educated and mature professional, I heavily identified with whatever went on in my mind. The idea that my thoughts were not the truth and my feelings weren't facts was revolutionary and gave me some headspace and freedom from my thought world. I could now separate my emotions from who I was as a person, and it opened me up to the possibility that I was much more than what I thought.

I sought out more information and clarity. The slam dunk came when I read Eckhart Tolle's *The Power of Now*. I was in the airport on my way to St. John, US Virgin Islands, and again came the truth: you are not who you think you are; who you are is beyond what you see, know, and feel. In *The Power of Now*, Tolle uncovers a profound distinction between the "self" as the perception of you formed in your mind for survival, and the "I am" as your true consciousness that has the power to create anything in the present moment. He shares his own deeply personal account of how intense suffering caused his *I am* to completely detach from identifying with his unhappy, suffering *self*, and allowed him to experience a state of true consciousness and spirit. His revelation resonated so deeply with me, I still get chills reading it. Knowing that I am the observer watching, being, and creating from a space free from identification with struggle, lack, or fear switched on the light of my spirit and then I knew I was limitless.

Reading those books planted the seed that became my declaration of I am Life-Changing Love. Today that declaration is still the context for how I define myself and my life. It clears the chaos and sets the tone and boundaries for what matters to me, how I want to live, and what impact I want to create. Life-Changing Love creates unlimited potential for who I can be, what I can do, and what I can accomplish and have. It's the origin and the starting point for my life that most aligns who we are as star stuff.

WHO ARE YOU BEING?

This is a slightly different question.

Who you are being is the way your star stuff shows up and shows out in the world. You channel the core energy of who you are through your being to engage with people and the world around you and experience life. You get to choose who you want to be and how you show up, and that is the number one lever you have to stake your claim and own your results and experiences.

If who you're being is aligned with what you want, you will create it with ease. If you show up in ways that don't align with what you truly want, you will likely struggle and create undesirable outcomes. How many times do you do everything you know to do and still end up having unfulfilling results? If doing the same thing expecting a different result is insanity, then being the same way trying to do something different is its own special flavor of insanity. It's not what you're doing, it's who you are and who you're being, that gives you access to the new results and experiences.

Just as your body has an anatomy, so does your being. It is the whole system of what you believe, what thought patterns you take on, your feelings and emotions, and what you choose to do or not do about them.

DISTINCTION: ANATOMY OF BEING

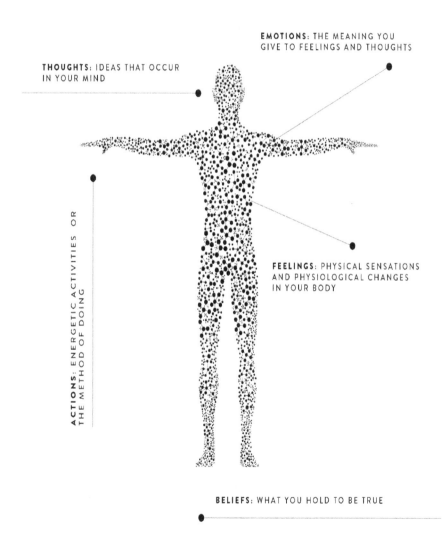

EMOTIONS: THE MEANING YOU GIVE TO FEELINGS AND THOUGHTS

THOUGHTS: IDEAS THAT OCCUR IN YOUR MIND

ACTIONS: ENERGETIC ACTIVITIES OR THE METHOD OF DOING

FEELINGS: PHYSICAL SENSATIONS AND PHYSIOLOGICAL CHANGES IN YOUR BODY

BELIEFS: WHAT YOU HOLD TO BE TRUE

Being is the source of how you create your life, and the anatomy of your being is the system that creates what your life looks like and how you experience it. Your anatomy of being is unique to you based on your perspective and view of life. Without clarity and ownership of who you're being, you will be at the effect or in reaction to your circumstances and the people around you. Your most valuable resources; time, energy, and peace of mind will be dictated by others.

Look at the results of your life. How do you relate to your family and friends? The world? Yourself? What experiences do you tend to have on a day-to-day basis? What things do you have and what's missing? Are you happy, miserable, curious, or passionate? There are all types of results in life from success, fulfillment, impact, and health, to having a family, a nice home, money, power, love, you name it! There are a million quotes, definitions, and descriptions about life, but what matters is which of life's results are meaningful to you. If you take an honest inventory of your results, you can connect the dots between who you are being and what you have.

HAVE-DO-BE

Most of us pursue life's results in a very clear pattern that goes like this … When I HAVE energy, money, time, love, etc. I will DO things like workout, travel, start a business, etc. and then I'll BE happy, free, at peace, etc. We look for what's missing in our being but then set goals for our having and doing to close the gap. How is that supposed to work? With HAVE-DO-BE you can accomplish and achieve many things but miss the whole experience of life in the process. Was it fun, were you free or joyful? Did you feel significant or impactful? Are you at peace? Many times the answer is no because your actions were being driven by a scarcity mentality to fill a void of what was missing. As a result, you miss out on the pleasure, peace, and joy of the journey. When you focus on creating your life from a space of fear and lack, your goals, vision boards, and bucket lists of everything you desire can trap you inside patterns of inspiration, empowerment, action and then exhaustion. You end up doing so much and not getting the results you truly desire.

Remember, I thought I would be happy and feel stable only after I had a good job, a home, a husband, and a family. So what did I do? I did all the right things to make that job, home, husband, and family happen. I worked hard in school, interned at great companies, stayed socially involved and active, and made smart choices. I knew what I wanted and was clear that this was the answer. I believed if I had all this, I would finally be stable and happy. Well it wasn't, and I wasn't, and I felt the exact opposite, stretched all over the place and miserable.

HAVE-DO-BE didn't work because it falsely attached my being happy and stable to a disconnected process of doing and having when the truth is pretty straightforward… being comes from being. Doing is not being, and having is not being. Both can inspire, support, cultivate, and even initiate a state of being but it is not sustainable. With HAVE-DO-BE you've got it backwards because being is actually the cause of doing and having, not the other way around.

BE-DO-HAVE

Now let's flip the script. You may or may not be familiar with the concept of BE-DO-HAVE. It's the basic idea that you create what you want by first choosing to BE happy, free, etc. then choosing to DO happy and free things that result in you HAVING experiences and results that happiness and freedom bring.

It's cause and effect. Who you are is a human being and a creator of your reality. You are already being some kind of way, and you're creating the exact match for that being all the time, even if you're unaware of it. When you're in BE-DO-HAVE alignment, you're being who you desire and creating powerfully and beautifully exactly what you want to experience. Think of your results in three parts; tangible possessions, personal experiences, and impact on others. Most importantly these results align with your deepest desires. They are meaningful and fulfilling in a way that matters to you most with the ultimate result of being your authentic self, living on purpose and positively impacting the lives of others. You can always look at the results you've created and see how aligned you are or aren't with your deepest desires.

With BE-DO-HAVE, you still enjoy achieving results and acquiring new things. However, when you focus on who you're being first, there is no gap. What matters to you and what results you accomplish will always line up. You'll experience exactly what's consistent with who you're being. This connection will increase your energy, and things that are unimportant will fall away. Sometimes they'll go with ease and sometimes with resistance but always with peace. When you not only choose, but first define and design the anatomy of who you're being and then start doing with conscious intention, the results are limitless and what you have will be right on target.

CHAPTER 2

BEPRINTING™

You don't get what you want, you don't even get what you believe, you create what you embody.

—Radiah Rhodes, Author

BEprinting is the process of blueprinting who you are being. It is a systematic practice of designing and aligning the anatomy of your being to intentionally create what you want. It's about living a whole life by optimizing your time, fueling your energy, and tapping directly into your own power to create experiences and transform any result.

I practice BEprinting to activate my shift from doing to being and keep myself consciously aligned and on purpose. I define, design, strategize and plan out my being, and then let go and live my life on my own terms. Every quarter I take a few hours to choose an area of focus and design my strategy for being. If I'm struggling or I get overwhelmed, my BEprint™ restores my awareness of who I am, and I can immediately create the shift I want. Each time I go through the process, I shift back into my core definition and design of my being which allows me to become my best self in each moment. I become conscious, present, confident, calmer, and peaceful. I communicate more powerfully. I ask for exactly what I want in all situations and experience it. I say no. I worry less about things outside of my control, and I focus on my passions. I lighten up, enjoy myself, and have fun. Life opens up, and my results, tangible, experiential, and impactful are off the charts!

SPIRIT + SCIENCE + REALITY = RESULTS

BEprinting combines spirit, science, and reality and gives you concrete tools to create tangible results on your own terms. Concepts like being have typically been spiritual conversations amongst gurus. Through authors like Eckhart Tolle, Don Miguel Ruiz, and Dr. Wayne Dyer, many people have become more aware and started engaging with these spiritual principles and truths. Today there are more mainstream conversations about our souls and how we are spiritual beings living a human experience. These truths aren't always completely understood, but they resonate deeply and open up new insights into our lives.

Beyond the spirit, you can test the physical world for scientific and practical clues as to how it all works. Books like Rhonda Byrne's The Secret and Steven R. Covey's *7 Habits of Highly Effective People* have helped us gain further understanding of the mechanics behind peaceful manifestation. Universal laws of attraction, abundance, vibration, and many others work hand in hand with the spiritual nature of our being to manifest things in the real world. The science gives us practical ways to tap into the spiritual truths and universal laws to navigate life successfully. Books, blogs, and seminars are filled with tips, and life hacks to implement techniques for self-defined success.

There has been significant positive impact on the quality of life from increasing awareness of the spirit and science, but what about our own personal realities? We all come from different backgrounds and circumstances that drive our existing mindsets yet most of the information and self-improvement tools on our radars don't take our unique anatomy of being into account. The details of your personal wiring and the fabric of your everyday life can be the largest factor between you and your success. However, solutions are typically presented as advice from top performers or a host of tactics, action plans, and to do lists that assume we are all equally positioned to execute, overlooking how much the differences in our realities matter.

Think of it this way. When you build a house, you have a vision (spirit). You also know there is a clear process and method for building a house (science), and that the space and land you choose are unique to your house's location (reality). All that said, you want the end result of your house to be exactly what you envision, and to ensure that outcome you use a blueprint. That blueprint includes the elevation, terrain, and landscape of your house's location. If that information is not considered as part of the design and building of your home, you can expect to see flooding, cracks in the foundation, and other major issues with the structure of the house. The blueprint is critical in that it considers the vision, the process, and the landscape of where the vision is to be built.

Your life is the same way, so BEprinting is about uncovering and clearly identifying who you're being and bringing spirit, science, and reality together to move you into your goal. This is a new and different conversation that is meant to expand and elevate your experience and results into a whole new space. Once your life is aligned with who you are—who you truly are—remember the star stuff, you'll experience authenticity, fulfillment, creativity, and things you once believed were impossible.

CHAPTER 3

CHECK YOUR INTENTION

Please take responsibility for the energy you bring into the space
—Dr. Jill Taylor Bolte, American Author and Speaker

Intention is one of the most significant parts of BEprinting. It is how we define or measure your being. Remember: everything is energy. Energy is constantly vibrating and resonating to, through, and from your being in the form of intention. The notion of *being* can seem vague or abstract and is generally characterized by an energy which you can't see, but you can feel. Measuring intention is a way of making this invisible world of energy visible, giving you the ability to powerfully design and create your outcomes.

When I hear the word intention, it's usually referring to what someone "meant" or "didn't mean" to happen in a given situation.

You'll say, "I didn't mean for that to happen," or "That wasn't my intention," as if intention is just a thought or a single and separate entity from who you are and how you show up in a situation.

Consider this twist on the definition, intention is the full energetic measure of who you are being at any moment. You don't have an intention. You are an intention. Intention is more than a beginning thought or objective of what you hope happens. It is a measure of the full intensity and type of energy you hold towards experiencing a specific result in the real world. Intention resonates with you as an attitude or belief about your power to create what you want. It also radiates from your being as a signal to others and the universe about who you are and the results you are creating.

Your intention is an exact match for the outcome and impact you create. When you experience a response you don't want or don't like, you were still intentional about what you created. You were just unaware of the full anatomy of your intention at the time. Just as the words you speak are only 7% of your communication, your outward actions are only a fraction of how people interact with you. Your internal world of energy can speak much louder than your actions. Your full anatomy is what engages with others, so when you get a result or response you don't want or like, check your intention. Who were you being? Don't just check your thoughts and actions. Check your full anatomy; your feelings emotions, and your underlying beliefs. They always leave clues as to exactly how your outcome was created. You are a shining light. The forces attracted to that shining beam are based on the anatomy of who you are being.

You create it all. It's all radiating from you as intention.

THE BEPRINT™ INTENTION SCALE

EXPERIENCE	ENERGETIC	LEVEL
SOVEREIGNTY Supreme power or authority to govern yourself. Being present and able to respond with power and confidence in any moment.	EMBODYING	7
SURRENDERING To cease resistance and relinquish control to a greater power. Acknowledging and aligning with truth.	KNOWING	6
	COMMITTING	5
SEEKING To go in search of, look for, or try to find. Stretching and expanding/ taking on new thoughts, actions, and responses to people or circumstances.	BELIEVING	4
	ASKING	3
STRIVING Make great efforts, try hard to achieve. Actively focusing energy to get or obtain something you don't yet possess or have.	WANTING	2
	WISHING	1
SETTLING Accept or agree to something you consider less than satisfactory, adopt security or comfort. Rationalizing away what you know to be true.	INDIFFERENCE	0
	RESIGNED	-1
SACRIFICING Killing off your gift or what you want for some noble cause. Habit of doing for others before doing for yourself. Isolating and busying yourself by over committing and taking on the demands and needs of others over your own.	AVOIDING	-2
	DENYING	-3
STRUGGLING Having difficulty getting an outcome, forcing or fighting to handle or cope. Going against "Truth" and repeating cycles of undesirable patterns.	RESISTING	-4
	SUPPRESSING	-5
SUFFERING Undergoing or enduring pain, illness, and hardship. Blaming (self or others). Indulging in emotions of anger or victim mindset.	RESENTING	-6
	SABOTAGING	-7

You Get What You Measure

Welcome to the BEprint™ Intention Scale. This is the actual *divine guide*. It is a truth-teller. This is your personal reality check that incorporates your spiritual truth, the science of living, and the circumstances of your reality.

This scale is the most clear and efficient tool I use to spark transformation. Having the ability to measure something as seemingly abstract as being, gives you significant power to transform and affect it. The scale is structured in multiple levels, so you can really get specific about who you're being and how you're showing up for something. As you look up and down the levels, you cannot help but see yourself somewhere on the scale. The awareness of where you are illuminates your reality, the possibilities, and your personal pathway to a result you desire. As soon as you see your level, you'll know where you're resonating, and will automatically start evaluating if it's where you want to be and how to shift to a new intention level that is purposeful and aligned with what you want.

The Scale ranges from level -7 up to level 7. Each level shows both your internal experience and the external energetic you're sending out to the universe as it relates to your desire or goal. Your experience captures the internal impact of how you relate to your goal inside your own world. While your energetic describes what you're actively doing and communicating externally to others as it relates to your goal.

Here's how you check your intention:

- Think about a vision, goal, result, or experience you desire.
- Get a clear picture in your mind and state your goal either out loud or in your mind as a thought.
- Take a deep breath and ask yourself, *Where am I on this scale as it relates to my goal?*
- Go level by level and ask yourself, *Am I suffering, resenting something, or sabotaging myself around it? Am I struggling or resisting the truth or requirements of my goal?*
- Go up and down the scale and read the descriptions until you hear and feel your answer rise up into your consciousness.
- If you stay open and light, you will know it. Be patient, it will come.
- Stay out of your head and in your heart.
- Be open to and willing to tell the truth.

Once you see your level, ask yourself, *Is where I'm resonating enough to be and live the way I desire?* If the answer is yes, you're there—keep being. However, I'd assert that if it were truly a *yes*, you'd already be experiencing what you want. So if the answer is no, ask yourself, *Where would I resonate to create what I want?*

Go back up and down the levels on the scale and choose a

place to start. It may be one level above where you are today, and that may be enough. Your intention can be the key as well as the lock to your goals. Just be willing to start somewhere.

For example, if your goal is to lose fifteen pounds, and you typically say *no* when someone asks you to exercise, or you've been all over the place trying different diets, you are likely at a negative level of intention. A flat-out no is somewhere between avoiding and resisting, which equals struggle and therefore not losing the weight.

Most of the time you're not aware of the energy behind your actions or the impact of your full intention on your results. You say, "I want to lose fifteen pounds, I really want to lose this weight." You know exactly what to do to lose weight, yet you resist taking the actions necessary to achieve the goal. What's the result? Struggling to lose weight because you are resisting the truth of who you'd have to become to lose it. How are you going to lose the weight? How can you possibly reach a goal by resisting it?

Uncovering that resistance, and telling the truth about it, is the first step to transforming your results. Becoming conscious and being specific about your intention gives you agency so you can affect your results more powerfully in an accelerated way.

Own Your Intention

Moving up the intention scale is a process, and in reality, we unconsciously move up and down the scale all the time. One moment you feel defeated or discouraged, and the next moment you feel hopeful and inspired. Each level is always available to you. Depending on where you are on the scale, you can feel an increase or decrease of peace and energy flowing through your spirit and your life.

Over time the up and down movement pulls you in and out of alignment with your goals and desires. The times when I'm most out of alignment are the most painful. I feel out of sync, my eating and sleeping patterns are off, and I get short tempered. The telltale sign for me is my morning routine. I wake up groggy, skip breakfast, miss workouts, and start snapping at my family for things like breathing too loudly. When you're unconsciously resonating at low levels of intention, you get off-center, it affects your well-being and everything around you. Your ability to be aware of and responsible for your intention level directly influences whether you have alignment or a gap between your reality and your desired results. It is your responsibility to own your intention and thus your experience of life.

As my uncle would say, "It's simple, but it ain't easy. "

The simple parts are all the knowns. You know your goal, you know what you want to create or experience. You know your intention level based on the BEprint™ Intention Scale. You also know the gap between your intention level and what level it takes to reach your goal. The hard part is, how the hell do you close the gap? How do you surrender and let go of your fear of betrayal when you're still suffering from the pain and struggling with the anger of the situation happening in the first place? How do you move from the sacrificing that goes with carrying, birthing, and nursing two babies in a twenty-four month period to the commitment of exercising regularly and proudly wearing a bikini on vacation? (That one sounded personal, didn't it?)

The power is in your consistency of tapping into a level and choosing conscious, deliberate and purposeful actions that align with your goal. You can't fool the universe, it sees and hears the authentic you loud and clear. You must embrace the process and align with your true intention to create the results you want because, without intention, you cannot fulfill your goals. My goal here is to clear up the fog and ambiguity on how to get what you want and to give you a repeatable method to see and understand who is really in your way.

Out of all the components of the BEprint™, I chose to write this book about intention, because it is the most profound and practical lever available to accelerate your shift from doing to being. Shifting your intention is the fast pass to owning your energy, time, and peace of mind. Throughout the rest of these pages, I am going to take you on a journey up The BEprint™ Intention Scale, to the ultimate life of passion, purpose, and fulfillment that is calling you!

PART II

DISCOVER

Discover is all about truth. It's about recognizing the pattern of who you've been all this time unconsciously and without awareness. It is acknowledging the whole truth beyond what you've suppressed, resisted, denied, avoided, or rationalized away to stay safe and comfortable.

The layers in Discover have been formed your whole life, and have been reinforced, yet undetected, for years. You will see the old foundation for what it is and excavate those layers before you lay a new foundation and build a new house. As you move through the intention levels of discover, you will find yourself becoming lighter and free. You'll let go of what no longer serves you and open up to the possibility of something new.

Chapter 4 | SUFFERING

THE ROOT OF SUFFERING IS ATTACHMENT.

— BUDDHA, FOUNDING FIGURE OF BUDDHISM

EXPERIENCE	ENERGETIC	LEVEL
How you are experiencing the energetic in your life	The energy or signal you're sending out to the universe.	
SUFFERING		
Undergoing or enduring pain, illness, and hardship. Blaming (self or others). Indulging in emotions of anger or victim mindset.	RESENTING	-6
	SABOTAGING	-7

THE ANATOMY OF SUFFERING

2. WHAT THOUGHTS WOULD I THINK?

WHY IS THIS HAPPENING TO ME? IT FEELS SO BAD, I CAN'T TAKE IT ANYMORE. I CAN'T BELIEVE I KEEP DOING THIS TO MYSELF. I AM BAD, WRONG, ASHAMED.

3. WHAT EMOTIONS WOULD I CLAIM?

DESPAIR, ABANDONMENT, BETRAYAL, TRAPPED, WEEPY.

4. WHAT FEELINGS WOULD I EXPERIENCE?

KNOT IN CHEST, STOMACH PAINS/ACIDITY, HEARTACHE, HEAVINESS, FATIGUE.

5. WHAT ACTIONS WOULD I TAKE AND NOT TAKE?

ISOLATE, RETREAT, SULK. NEGLECT RESPONSIBILITIES, RUMINATE,

WHAT BELIEFS WOULD I HOLD TRUE?

I'M ALL ALONE. I AM NOT ENOUGH.

How many of us are doing this to our lives? Sabotaging our relationships, our bodies, or our spirit. Resenting circumstances we don't control. When something feels painful, I reread this definition and ask myself, "Where in your life are you repeatedly enduring pain, illness, or hardship blaming yourself or others and indulging in anger and a victim mind-set?"

A LOVE STORY

For most of my twenties, I was carefree and having fun. I graduated with an engineering degree from a great school … #packproud! I landed the engineer's dream job at a Fortune 100 corporation, and I moved to a city where my best friend and a host of good girlfriends lived. Plus, to top it all off, my boyfriend, Calvin, now my husband, had moved to the same area about three months earlier.

It was the perfect beginning, and everything was flowing smoothly. I don't think I even noticed all the changes happening. It seemed like I woke up one day and hated my job, couldn't stand my roommate another day, and Calvin and I were forever arguing. It must have been a slow decline because I can't point to any one incident that happened, but I could feel myself going into overdrive grasping for solutions. Like clockwork, I went into my superhero mode of doing to avoid what I didn't want to face. I replaced my 1989 Toyota with no air conditioning and a trunk that filled with water when it rained with my first new car. It was a jet-black Volkswagen with fewer than ten miles on it. Then, I bought a beautifully rehabbed row home across from a historical museum and fewer than five minutes from the inner harbor.

Things were looking good, my commute to work was smoother, and I finally had my own space without the roommate tension. However, I still felt like I was slipping. I was excited by all the newness, but the core problems still remained. Buying a new car and new house did little about the woes at my job and in my relationship. In fact, buying a new car raised eyebrows at work, and Calvin ended up resenting that I had bought my first house without involving him.

That was the start of desperately trying to survive the realization that things were not turning out the way I had hoped. How could reuniting with my close friends, starting a career, making money, and being with my boyfriend be problematic? At that point, those questions didn't matter because regardless of how or why, it was a problem. The solid life I had built was now in serious jeopardy, and I was terrified of the pain of loneliness and abandonment I associated with instability.

Nothing was working out, and I found myself scrambling to escape the pain. The less stable things felt, the more desperate I behaved and the more I suffered. What started out beautiful—a rehabbed row home in a revitalized area of the city—ended up a liability of repairs and expenses that I refused to address. I became a victim at work: complaining, judging, and feeling completely victimized by whatever issues and barriers I faced. I spent money irresponsibly and didn't save a dime, other than my company's contribution to retirement. And as you can imagine, my most insane behavior was in my love life.

Here's the story. Calvin and I had dated for the better part of six years. Zero talk of marriage, just friendship, fun, and easy. Then the drama of my home repairs, work life, and money kicked in looking like my life wasn't going to turn out well, so I went into hyper drive.

ENTER SELF-SABOTAGE

My self-sabotage begins like a problem solver gone wild. Calvin calls me a yellow jacket because when I lock onto something, it's as if I keep stinging and biting it, and never let up. That's exactly who I became about marriage, and it was a hot mess. I had us in relationship counseling on my insurance, while we were still only dating. I left my house in shambles three to four days a week to drive thirty minutes and live out of a bag at his house only to then drive almost an hour to work every day. What the f$*k? I was crazy, and this went on for years.

Then finally it happened.

We got engaged. That was the goal, right? Awesome, right? No. We had no wedding date, and every planning decision was like pulling teeth. I had a beautiful diamond, but beyond that, nothing was happening. It was another life not turning out the way I had hoped moment that sent me even deeper into sabotage.

At this point, nothing could describe the depths of my addiction to solving the problem of getting to the altar. We went back to counseling, looked at a million venues, interviewed vendors, and anything else I could force on the wedding checklist. I kept thinking, Why is this so hard?

At one point I thought, Maybe he's on drugs or something. Seriously, I'm not kidding. I was losing it, desperately slipping trying to survive the reality that this man did not want to marry me.

That was it. He was not going to marry me. In fact, it wasn't even about me. He wasn't interested in getting married at all. That was the truth I couldn't and wouldn't accept let alone face that had me in full sabotage mode. The pain and shame of that reality was too great, and I fought it off with everything I had. I was deliberately sabotaging the truth, damaging myself, and obstructing reality for fear of an unstable life that felt like a failure. At the time, I wasn't conscious of that fear but found myself deep in the throes of fighting it.

I would have never said I was suffering or sabotaging anything.

From my perspective, I was fighting for what was "supposed to be" and what was destined. I had no idea how my whole energy and my actions were undermining my true desire. My desperation was literally causing more instability and actually pushing Calvin away.

If you let me tell it at the time: I was committed, faithful, kind, went out of my way to be supportive and had earned the right for things to go the way I wanted. When they didn't, I lost all reason and started to sabotage myself, and my own spirit. I finally hit bottom, when I busted out crying one night because he didn't notice my new hair color. Clearly, that wasn't the issue, but my soul couldn't take it anymore. In a pure moment of surrender, I gave back the ring, broke off our engagement, and let it all go. It was frightening and paralyzing at the same time.

Self-sabotage is coping on steroids. It is usually an unconscious and hyperactive reaction to a perceived threat to your livelihood or identity. It's where you default when shit gets real, and you don't like what you see happening. It is the lowest level of intention because it is vehemently working against what you really want, even when it seems like it's fighting for it. When you self-sabotage, you resent reality and truth. In a state of sabotage, you are committed to your fears and ego for survival. My flavor of self-sabotage drove me to desperation, and left me feeling empty, lost, and humiliated.

The internal experience of self-sabotage is suffering. My repeated frantic attempts to fight off instability ate away at my self-esteem, hope, passion, and vision for my life. I suffered through the ups and downs for years and went through depression and anxiety even after I stopped the sabotaging behaviors. I had damaged my spirit to the point where I had no joy. I went through gut-wrenching anxiety, lost thirty pounds, and shut everything out for months. I felt embarrassed and lost all hope of creating a stable and full life.

The only remedy to my suffering proved to be patience and self-compassion. When I broke off our engagement, it wasn't a ploy to trick Calvin into changing. I thought I was giving up my only chance for a happy life. It was real and painful, so I let go of what was happening outside of my control. I realized I had to focus on the one thing that I could control; me. I concentrated on every action I could take and every act of love I could give myself. The more I did this, moment by moment, my spirit was restored.

Because of self-compassion, I could be still and rest. I could mourn what I felt I had lost. Once I got still and took care of myself, the world opened up. What followed was choice and freedom. I reconnected to what I loved, working out, traveling, and pure fun. I was in my twenties and loved a good party. I had given all that up while trying so hard to get married and avoid a failed life. I brought sexy back with a vengeance, yet another thing I had forgotten about myself during my obsessed period.

Restoring what I had diminished in myself took time, forgiveness, patience, and faith. I focused on remembering who I was and nurturing myself. I started to immerse myself in prayer, church, family, and friends ... eventually, over time, not only was I restored, I evolved.

I was better, stronger, and wiser.

Since I mentioned that Calvin is now my husband, I should also say that after about a year, we reconnected by *coincidence*. The time apart had done us well and allowed significant growth in both of us. We slowly built a new relationship, and here we are today with two children, and over ten years of marriage. In hindsight, it was clear that I mistook marriage for eternal stability. So as I sit here in my tenth-year of marriage just thinking that makes me burst out laughing. I'm just glad I can laugh!

SHIFTING TO BEING

A moment of self-compassion can change your entire day. A string of such moments can change the course of your entire life.

—Christopher Germer, bestselling author of the *Mindfulness Solution*

Be a compassionate nurturer to yourself. When you're suffering, care and kindness are needed. See where you're hurting and be kind to yourself. Become your own best friend, and be patient with yourself. When I feel that frantic tinge of suffering start, I sit with myself and say, "It's okay, I got you. You're all right." I say what I might want someone else to say, what I might want my husband or kids to say, and I let it soothe my soul. I become exactly who or what I'm longing for at that moment. I take as long as I need to nurture myself and restore my peace and security.

Arrange your time, energy, and attention around what restores you; mind, body, and spirit. Fill your schedule with acts of self-care and compassion. Block regular time in your calendar specifically devoted to your wellbeing. Whether it's two minutes to stop and take deep breaths or getting into action and working out, getting a massage, or sitting at the bookstore. Choose what works for you and create a daily ritual or regimen that gives you peace of mind and allows you to focus on restoring yourself. Acknowledge each small act of self-care as an example of your strength. Make it an affirmation of who you are. As you are restored, begin to acknowledge the choice and ability you have to take good and loving care of yourself and rewrite your narrative. Reach out for support and accountability to keep you moving forward and create a structure to stay consistent.

My schedule changes drastically with the seasons. About every quarter, the kids' sports practices, client activity, or the holiday calendar seems to shift everything around. Last year, I learned how suffering can impact your body the hard way. I had developed a habit of loading my schedule with back to back obligations to avoid the reality of my day job. I went into superhero mode, and in keeping with my default pattern of *doing a whole lot,* I set up a life support system of medical appointments just to keep it together. I spent more than a year ignoring my doctor's direction to slow down and change my schedule until chronic fatigue syndrome, and an autoimmune system reaction sat me down for months.

I could no longer keep doing *the most* with so little self-care. I had to get real with myself and shift my priorities to center everything else around my health and specific activities to feed my well-being.

Step one, implement my exit strategy to finally remove my major stressor and exit my day job. For me, this was a long time coming, and the universe presented an opportunity to move on that I couldn't refuse.

Next, was to restore alignment with my purpose and passion. I'm a planner and a wellbeing innovator, so I leveraged my creativity and designed a personal practice to keep me whole and well. I sit down with a quarterly calendar, and a weekly schedule template, to chart out my sleeping habits including my morning ritual and my wind down routine. I choose a couple of fitness and relaxation activities and create a wellness regimen. I map out key business milestones, and I confirm my travel plans, plus all the holidays. I lay it all out into a standing weekly schedule with my well-being as the priority.

Now, do I follow it? I'd say about 60% to 70% of the time. The rest is life showing up. The point is, I have a clear north star to follow when chaos comes at me. I know what windows of time I have for spontaneous meeting requests and I can play or rest without worrying about dropping the proverbial ball. This is my go-to ritual to live a vibrant and healthy life, not just keep it together.

Chapter 5 | STRUGGLING

EXPERIENCE	ENERGETIC	LEVEL
How you are experiencing the energetic in your life	The energy or signal you're sending out to the universe	

STRUGGLING	RESISTING	-4
Having difficulty getting an outcome, forcing or fighting to handle or cope. Going against "Truth" and repeating cycles of undesirable patterns.	SUPPRESSING	-5

THE ANATOMY OF STRUGGLING

2. WHAT THOUGHTS WOULD I THINK?
IT'S TOO HARD. I'M CONFUSED, I DON'T
KNOW WHAT TO DO. HERE WE GO AGAIN.

3. WHAT EMOTIONS WOULD I CLAIM?
FRUSTRATED, DISAGREEABLE, TENSE,
ULTRA SENSITIVE.

4. WHAT FEELINGS WOULD I EXPERIENCE?
BLOCKED FEELING IN THROAT AND CHEST.
BACK, NECK AND SHOULDER TENSION,
CLENCHED FISTS AND JAWS

5. WHAT ACTIONS WOULD I TAKE AND NOT TAKE?
DEFEND YOURSELF
VIGOROUSLY,WHINE AND COMPLAIN,
INCONSISTENT ACTION

WHAT BELIEFS WOULD I HOLD TRUE?
LIFE IS TOUGH. I CAN'T WIN.

The reality is, life will require you to deal with trials and tough situations. It will force you to put forth the effort and be subsequently tested. Circumstances will challenge you and persisting and dealing with difficulty can give meaning and purpose to life especially when there's a lot at stake. The more your circumstances require you to stretch, the more you are likely to struggle at some point in time. Stretching outside of your comfort zone puts you in new and uncertain spaces where you have little to no experience. The natural response is to find something familiar or relatable to get your bearings. Navigating the time and discomfort between unfamiliar and familiar can become an exhausting fight, and struggling can become a habit of overcoming as the badge of survival.

MY STRUGGLE

I worked for the same company for eighteen years. I know, who does that? For me the cycle of struggle became predictable. Every new assignment or manager brought with it some strife and struggle. Each time I adjusted to their style of work, requirements, and preferences. I barely knew who I was and the constant changes made it difficult to see the truth that I was the square peg trying to fit into a round hole.

I'm a creative being. I have an entrepreneurial spirit. At the time, I didn't know it because I was suppressing it. As a result of my life experiences, I valued loyalty, stability, and achievement more than freedom, creativity, and expression. For security, I needed my value to constantly be validated and confirmed. So I suppressed my truth to fit the mold, be valued, and survive.

My company had a strong culture of loyalty and a high value of excellence, which was right up my alley. Given my childhood, you could see how it gave me the sense of security I needed. I became attached to it. There was no separation between the company and my identity, so when things felt unstable at work, I struggled— hard. What I saw as bad assignments, weak bosses, delayed promotions, and petty colleagues triggered constant turmoil, which I internalized as failure and inadequacy. All of it threw me for a loop and exhausted me in the process.

My struggle was driven by fear. Fear of judgment from my colleagues and managers, which in my mind, could destroy my reputation of excellence I had built over time. My track record of achievement being damaged and jeopardized was the ultimate threat to my stability. Who would I be if I wasn't excellent, if I didn't have this job, or do this work, in this specific way? What would I do, and what would it mean to me if I acknowledged I didn't fit in?

It was a vicious cycle, and each time I made it through one obstacle, there was another one to overcome right behind it. After years of the same thing, I figured out that overcoming was overrated, and I stopped the struggle. I just gave it up.

At first, I was tired and had no fight left, so I said f&#$ it and let it go. I never realized how much I was suppressing myself. I got bold and diverted my attention to what I personally valued, was passionate about, and believed I could influence. This helped me restore my energy, and soon after that, I started to build my true nature as a creative and an entrepreneur.

I was optimistic about finding an outlet at work to impact, but as I could have predicted, the struggle was waiting around the corner. This time it was a judgment of my style. I was told I had too much confidence and could be intimidating. I was also told that a couple of colleagues felt I didn't accept negative information. They were right. As a project manager, issues come up all the time. From my lens, issues didn't equate to negativity, and I never doubted or questioned my team's ability to solve any challenge. My responses lacked drama, and I didn't commiserate, so I was labeled as being disengaged and unavailable. All code for you're not being who we think you should be. It became a full assault on my character and capability, tempting me to start down the old path of resisting in the form of defending myself, but I stopped. I was over it.

Struggling had taken its toll. My family had been impacted by my stress, my health declined significantly, and my quality of life was diminished. I realized every time I engaged in fighting someone's opinion or judgment of me, I was validating it in some way. Even slightly engaging it fed the mania and sent a destructive message that it was true on some level. It was self-defeating and painful. Just being in the environment was a threat to my identity, and I struggled, fighting for my freedom to be the creative entrepreneur I had become for myself or succumb to who they wanted me to be to fit in.

I had to confront the truth. I was not a fit. I had been conditioned to believe that not being a fit meant something was wrong with me. That this me I had created trying to fit in all those years was incompetent, not valuable, and therefore would be let go of, and lose security.

I had to forgive myself for giving so much without regard for my own values and boundaries. I had to forgive my company for taking every bit of what I gave freely. Who wouldn't? It took this mental shift for me to build confidence in my new identity, passion, and truth. I became willing to let go of the old and see how what I was stepping into was far more valuable and promising than what I was releasing. I was literally and authentically done, and since the universe cooperates with a made-up mind, it burst wide open to move me forward!

We're conditioned to struggle, we glorify it, and we identify with it. The more you struggle, the stronger you're perceived to be. We're taught struggle is necessary for growth, hearing things like: if there is no struggle, there is no progress. We end up believing your struggle, and even how you struggle, says something about your toughness. It defines your worth.

Historically and culturally, struggle has been honored and celebrated. Struggles for freedom, equality, and justice are the cornerstones of respect and pride. Society recognizes struggle as necessary, even ordained in some cases. Overcoming struggle means you have the grit and perseverance to be successful.

Right? I know you're saying right. But is it?

What exactly is struggle? Is it good or bad? Is it necessary or not? The definition of struggle is fighting, forcing, resisting, and making strenuous or violent efforts to escape or get free of restraint. In other words, struggle is beast mode! When you struggle, there is something that you must fight for to survive. It is an all-out effort to save yourself from an imminent threat or danger to your very freedom.

Good, bad, necessary, or not—our view of struggle—is relative. What matters is struggle has an impact. When you read the definition, you automatically feel the intense stress. The pressure from the struggle can break you. Think about it. Fighting, resisting, forcing, and strenuous violent effort requires significant energy. Energy that is not sustainable. When struggle is employed for a short period of time, for a specific purpose, the outcome can be real growth. You can find victory in the triumph of your struggle. But when struggling persists over an extended period and is not clearly focused toward a specific end, it drains your resources dry.

Personally, my greatest struggle is right when I'm closest to my most powerful personal truth. In my past career, my real life of creativity, passion, and the freedom to be me had been calling for a long time. My pain and fear of losing the security I had identified with for so long was too threatening, so I was forced to suppress and resist it.

It's different for everyone. Your truth knocks at the door, and something inside you says, "Ahhhh, yes, that's it." Not even a second later, something else says, "Hold up! If that's the truth, then …," and all these ideas flood in. I'm going to have to quit my job, divorce my husband, or do something equally drastic.

All the while the truth is still knocking, and then it starts jiggling the door handle a little bit. It just gets louder and louder. The struggle begins when you start blocking the door. Or you start pulling on the handle to keep the door closed. Now … here you are on the side with all this stuff that no longer serves you, and you're struggling to keep the door closed because you're afraid of what's going to happen when that door opens, and the truth comes in.

Even though part of you knows the truth always gets in.

This can go on for years, creating a mind-set that identifies with hardship, so you keep fighting unconsciously until it becomes impossible to see good things happening without a struggle.

When people pursue big goals, you hear them say the struggle is real, which means they're trying and trying, but can't seem to break through to the result. There isn't necessarily any danger that requires a fight, but they're in a battle for this new and big thing they want. Think about it, when you're working toward a new goal that requires you to step outside your comfort zone there's some fear or anxiety. You're taking bold new actions, and now there's a threat … to your ego, your confidence, and maybe even your reputation.

Being uncomfortable and bold, taking new actions, and feeling fear don't equate to struggle. You introduce struggle when you resist the reality of what's presently happening in the situation. The truth. You're afraid; you've never done this before; you could really use some help; your colleagues and family don't agree with what you're saying. These are some of the truths you might suppress and resist that keep you struggling. When you equate difficulty or discomfort with struggle, you immediately increase the effort and time needed to progress through the situation. It brings frustration and a destructive energy that undermines your intention. It will block your progress. Halt your momentum.

An alternative is to allow what's happening to happen. Watch it objectively, free from past fears and future attachments. Then determine how you can best respond. Work with what's really happening to reach your desired outcome. If you are willing to give up trying to force your struggle onto the situation, the universe can open up naturally, providing for you with a clear next step and ease. But first, you must be willing to release the fight.

SHIFTING TO BEING

Don't let your struggle become your identity.
—Unknown

Be vulnerable. Open yourself up and be willing to acknowledge the fullness of what you're experiencing. Consider what's working and what's not, what feels good, and what feels painful. Account for the light and the dark of your own thoughts and actions as well as others and allow yourself to see, hear, and speak the truth in a situation. Feel the uncertainty and allow yourself the space to be still without doing anything about it.

Be forgiving of yourself and others for what you believe has been done to you and let go of the pain you're holding inside. Letting go of the fight has an instantaneous effect. In some moments I can feel myself pushing, harping, and lasering in on my target ... for what? Usually to win a point, be right, and save face as a way to avoid fear, guilt, or shame.

Do you want to be happy or right—isn't that the saying? I choose happy. At some point, I hit my struggle limit, and that was enough for me. Between work, marriage, and children I got to a point where I believed my struggle dues had been paid.

Happy or right? I choose happy. I choose happy so hard, I can be in full verbal assassin mode and lay down my weapon just like that. I stop talking, stop resisting, stop fighting right then and there. I breathe that struggle energy right out of my system because I am not committed to struggling. I am committed to peace, ease, and flow. It is that simple and at that moment I'm free, I'm light, and I'm happy to move on to the next moment with my dignity, respect, and confidence intact. What I'm really putting down is my fear and anxiety of being wrong, disrespected, found out, or any other threat that can drive me to resist the truth of the moment. When I allow myself to see what's really happening beyond my fear, I can see there's no threat and let it go. It comes down to choosing happy, peace, and ease without letting the fear of losing my ego self-drive me to fight and struggle. I will live happy, peacefully, joyfully, and free especially in moments of fear, anger, and shame.

Acknowledge your fear and speak it out loud to yourself and others. Share how you feel regardless of how uncomfortable it may be. Say no, ask for help, and engage in conversations seeking answers and understanding. Allow things out of your control to process, and take steps to move or be guided to a better result. Believe in your truth without proving, defending, or justifying and be committed to showing up in peace as who you want to be. Right or happy? Stay present and flexible at the moment. Be conscious of what is really happening in the now, keeping your fears from past experiences or hopes for future outcomes from taking over the present.

Chapter 6 | SACRIFICING

*YOU'RE NOT REQUIRED TO SET YOURSELF ON FIRE TO KEEP OTHER
PEOPLE WARM.*

— UNKNOWN

EXPERIENCE	ENERGETIC	LEVEL
How you are experiencing the energetic in your life	The energy or signal you're sending out to the universe.	
SACRIFICING		
Killing off your gift or what you want for some noble cause. Habit of doing for others before doing for yourself. Isolating and busying yourself by over committing and taking on the demands and needs of others over your own.	**AVOIDING**	-2
	DENYING	-3

THE ANATOMY OF SACRIFICING

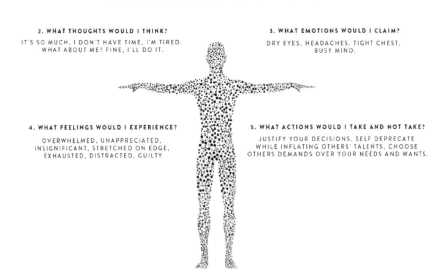

2. WHAT THOUGHTS WOULD I THINK?
IT'S SO MUCH, I DON'T HAVE TIME, I'M TIRED.
WHAT ABOUT ME? FINE, I'LL DO IT.

3. WHAT EMOTIONS WOULD I CLAIM?
DRY EYES, HEADACHES, TIGHT CHEST,
BUSY MIND.

4. WHAT FEELINGS WOULD I EXPERIENCE?
OVERWHELMED, UNAPPRECIATED,
INSIGNIFICANT, STRETCHED ON EDGE,
EXHAUSTED, DISTRACTED, GUILTY

5. WHAT ACTIONS WOULD I TAKE AND NOT TAKE?
JUSTIFY YOUR DECISIONS, SELF DEPRECATE
WHILE INFLATING OTHERS' TALENTS, CHOOSE
OTHERS DEMANDS OVER YOUR NEEDS AND WANTS.

WHAT BELIEFS WOULD I HOLD TRUE?
IT'S NO BIG DEAL. IT'S OK, I'M FINE.

Welcome to sacrificing, a graduation from suffering and struggling where your progress is worthy of acknowledgment but can still cause concern.

At sacrificing, you've inched up the scale a bit further. You started with suffering, enduring and indulging deep pain. Then you moved up a little bit to struggling, which has some power and movement in resisting, but is still negative since it is pushing away from your true desires. Still moving up the scale, you arrive at sacrificing.

When you sacrifice, you give up suppressing, and start to acknowledge that you actually have passions of your own that could use some nurturing. You open yourself up to experience some of what you want. However, the cup only stays half full because you pour out to others before you've fulfilled your own needs and desires.

Sacrificing is killing off your passion, gift, or goal for a justified cause.

Let's say you love writing and want to birth a book … someday. You finally sit down to write, and the kids come in and interrupt you because they're hungry. What do you do? You get up and feed the kids. They're your kids, and they gotta eat, right? Justifiable reason to stop at that moment, right? You'll get back to it, right? Passion sacrificed … *right?* Right.

You are right. Your children do have to eat. The moment of sacrifice showed up when it never occurred to you that there were options to both feed the children *and* write your book. Win-win scenarios are far from wishful thinking, but you'll miss the setup, if you're already defeated and habitually sacrificing.

Prioritizing life's responsibilities, from doctor's appointments to family visits to work deadlines are all very justifiable choices to make. However, each act of justification undermines your passion and true desire, and then they start to snowball. You've acknowledged what you want, but you deny yourself the time and space to go after it and experience it. By default, you're avoiding your passion or purpose. Why? Stepping into your passion and purpose is unknown territory which can be confronting and uncomfortable and meeting others' needs is familiar and safe.

The layers of your passion and purpose are unique to you, and by definition, anything unique to you can cause you to stand out, potentially drawing people's opinions and judgment. The more authentic you become, living your own personal path and truth, the more susceptible you are to judgment. Sacrificing is a noble, reasonable, and justifiable way to avoid that exposure.

MY SACRIFICE

Four years ago I decided to become an entrepreneur after being an employee for damn near twenty-five years. Essentially, I made a declaration to be an entrepreneur and this decision immediately created a major conflict between myself and my environment. As a seasoned employee, I knew my job from every angle, had enviable flexibility, and could predict my schedule for most weeks. As a startup entrepreneur, my world can be all over the place. The work and preparation never stop, and prospects can show up at any time.

I was following up on a lead from a small business conference and had scheduled a huge meeting for the second Friday of the month. I was excited and started clearing the calendar to make way for the birth of a major opportunity. I set up my schedule for the week including work time, in office time, kids' appointments, meetings, tennis, administrative work, and a family visit.

No sooner than I hit save on my calendar did the conflicts show up and the opportunities for sacrificing begin.

Kids' summer camp plans fell through—*okay, I'll take days off work and take on primary coverage for the week.*

Calvin scheduled critical client meetings, and our sitter was not available—*okay, I'll cancel tennis to cover the kids.*

Commute delays caused drop off and pick up changes—*okay, I'll pick up.*

Family visit impacted our morning routine—*okay, I'll go to work late to help get things in order.*

Calvin's meeting with the accountant ran late—*okay, I'll handle the kids getting ready for their sports practices.*

A friend called in need at a time when I need to get this proposal done—*okay, I'll answer the phone and talk for an hour.*

The list went on and on, and by now you can see how all of this added up. By Wednesday I had no patience. I was stressed from juggling kids, family, and work emails to stay above water. By Thursday I was exhausted. I started to feel physically sick and worried about whether I'd make it to my business meeting on Friday.

Then the guilt set in. By Friday I was pissed and worried that by being rushed, feeling tired and sick, I had "sacrificed" my ability to show up well at my meeting. Add to that, when I finally got on the highway, late because I had forgotten to make a hair appointment and had to unexpectedly rescue my hair at the last minute, there was stop-and-go traffic. I was ready to scream my head off in that car! I was going from Baltimore through Washington DC to Virginia at 5:00 p.m. on a Friday for a 6:00 p.m. meeting.

I felt the panic and defeat rising, so I called my partner Dr. Roni to talk me off the ledge. First, she declared that the traffic was going to move, and I was going to be at my meeting on time because it was destiny, and she said so. That's how Dr. Roni rolls. Then we deconstructed the week and shined the light on how all the sacrifices I had made brought me to the point of panic and defeat just before this big opportunity.

We talked for an hour, and I literally pulled up to the hotel at exactly 6:00 p.m. feeling light, free of worry, and ready to roll. I nailed the meeting.

Here's what we discovered. As a business professional, an entrepreneur, the wife of an entrepreneur, a mother of two, and an all-around active person, sacrificing is a slow death waiting in the wings to drain the very life out of me. I want to do what's best for my family. I want to keep the peace. However, most of the time, I'm simply tired. So each conflict that arises makes it's easy to choose the path of least resistance by sacrificing, which usually means handling everything myself.

Inside of a busy life, sacrifice is a downward spiral of justifying with a cumulative effect. The more you sacrifice, the easier it becomes, until it's automatic. You start to feel defeated, so you give up and do it again. Each time you choose to sacrifice, it takes a little of your spirit from you. To feel better, you spend energy showing and proving how right and noble your sacrificial choices are until you start believing them yourself. The needs of others become more important than your own and denying your own needs becomes a noble act, making you a silent and angry martyr.

Sacrificing is not as obvious and aggressive as flat out resisting something. You take a much more passive approach by simply avoiding and denying your truth for a very *good* reason. It's the invisible undermining of your goals, hidden behind doing something good or necessary for someone else. You're not telling your desires, "No way. I'm not doing that!" Instead, you'd say, "I'd love to do that!" or, "I wish I could, but unfortunately, I can't right now. I have this huge project at work that takes all my time."

Do you see how reasonable that sounds? Subtle and honorable but has the same impact of undermining your goals in the end.

As a human, you're wired for survival: fight, flight, or freeze. A perceived danger (including mental or emotional discomfort) can drive you to avoid pain at all costs. The goal of each of the negative intention levels is to keep you small and therefore safe. Sacrificing is a subtle and sophisticated way of staying safe. It's defensible and respectable, it's like putting a pretty bow on your survival mode

SHIFTING TO BEING

Freedom lies in being bold.
—Robert Frost

Be bold and brave. Reignite the connection between you and your core values. Take account of what you love and what matters to you and stand for it. Let go of martyrdom and assuming automatic responsibility for solving every issue and closing every gap. Give up justifying and own choosing what works for you without complaint. Be clear about your values and priorities and choose accordingly. Let your values guide and strengthen you as you boldly and bravely begin to show up consistently and in alignment with your beliefs.

I found something that makes me bold. My values of health and wellbeing. When I reconnected with this value, playing tennis was the activity that rose to the top of my priority list. I have a love affair with tennis. It is all about me. It fills me up. I play how I want when I want, and my energy goes all the way up!

Tennis gave me the first all-to-myself, guilt-free, and bold *NO* I had in a long time. You need me to stay late? *No, I have tennis.* You need me to run an errand? *No, I have tennis.* You need me to cover the kids' day off? *No, where's the sitter? I have tennis.* I didn't stop there. I used my tennis *NO* as practice to develop other *NOs*. *NOs*, that may not have been reasonable or justifiable to others. *NOs* because I said so and because they honored my values. Values are so important. They are what keep us on track and ensure our internal and external worlds align. They are a foundational part of how we define ourselves. Honoring our values builds our esteem by anchoring and affirming our identity.

When you choose to prioritize and honor yourself after a long period of sacrificing, it will shock the people around you. It's likely you have trained them to get their needs met before and beyond your own. Not only are they used to you putting them first, they like it, and they benefit from it. Don't get me wrong they're not deliberately minimizing your needs and wants, they've been following your lead, and now you are changing the game, and they'll have to adjust. It will take boldness to break that pattern and cycle that keeps interrupting your personal flow of progress towards your goals. When conflicts come up with the potential of sacrificing my tennis time, I have no issue being bold and saying "No. I'm not missing tennis." Each and every time I stick to my priority and honor health I become more and more unshakeable in the face of conflicts and pushback.

Once you take the bold step to show up different, bravery steps in to help keep you consistent while you retrain those around you. Being brave feels like exhilaration and danger at the same time.

When I'm on that court, I am affirmed for prioritizing my health and wellbeing. I get excited about it, and I'm compelled to share my love for tennis and commitment to health with others. Find your *tennis* and stay the course, stand for what you value and feel the freedom and excitement of living it and letting the world know about it.

Chapter 7 | SETTLING

YOUR PLAYING SMALL DOES NOT SERVE THE WORLD. THERE IS NOTHING ENLIGHTENED ABOUT SHRINKING SO THAT OTHER PEOPLE WON'T FEEL INSECURE.

— MARIANNE WILLIAMSON, AMERICAN SPIRITUAL TEACHER

EXPERIENCE	ENERGETIC	LEVEL
How you are experiencing the energetic in your life	The energy or signalyou're sending out to the universe.	

SETTLING	INDIFFERENCE	0
Accept or agree to something you consider less than satisfactory, adopt security or comfort. Rationalizing away what you know to be true.	RESIGNED	-1

THE ANATOMY OF SETTLING

2. WHAT THOUGHTS WOULD I THINK?
I CAN LIVE WITH THIS. IT'S ALL GOOD, IT'S JUST NOT IN THE CARDS.

3. WHAT EMOTIONS WOULD I CLAIM?
UNSURE, BLAH, MINIMAL EMOTIONS, THINGS COULD GO EITHER WAY.

4. WHAT FEELINGS WOULD I EXPERIENCE?
NUMB, OUT OF TOUCH WITH YOUR BODY.

5. WHAT ACTIONS WOULD I TAKE AND NOT TAKE?
DISENGAGE, DISCONNECT, DO NOTHING, RATIONALIZE SITUATIONS INTO STATUS QUO, STEP OVER YOUR EMOTIONS AND REACTIONS.

WHAT BELIEFS WOULD I HOLD TRUE?
I CAN'T DO OR HAVE ANY BETTER THAN THIS. I DON'T NEEDMUCH, THIS IS GOOD ENOUGH.

Settling is the turning point. It's right in the middle of the scale where you can be on your way up, on your way down, or stay square in the middle. It has a certain status quo effect and indifference that could go either way. You've already seen the path down the scale, and settling is a step up, in that you are no longer *actively* working against yourself.

Settling can be one of the most insidious levels of intention because there's no obvious or easily identified problem, although the whispers of what you really want are always there nagging you. However, because you've decided to settle, you start rationalizing, a lighter form of justifying, to quiet the internal noise and keep your passion from disturbing the peace.

Over time you become detached from your desires. They are always there, and you know it, however you're resigned to the notion of doing anything about it. You're comfortable, secure, maybe even content, and it's working for you. I call settling the intellectual's method of staying small because the rationales are usually brilliant. I know from experience.

On the flip side, you may develop a dissatisfaction with the status quo, and be compelled to act. The calling of your desire may get loud enough to start pulling you up the scale, or the void of passion and desire may push you down the scale to sacrificing, struggling, or suffering.

SETTLING FOR LESS

At a low point, I was very dissatisfied with my career and was going through a personal crisis at the same time. I had just gotten married, had two children, moved three times, built a house, and changed job assignments twice in twenty-four months. It was a two year period of major change, and I felt completely out of my mind constantly sacrificing, struggling, and suffering.

Occasionally there were stretches of time where I would come up out of the storm for air. The universe would give me a timeout so I could settle for a bit. I didn't have enough energy to travel further up the intention scale toward what I wanted, but I had exhausted my energy at the bottom levels. To keep my head above water, I rationalized that what I wanted was too big, and there was no way I could do it under the current circumstances. Life was good, I had so much to be grateful for, and here I was complaining. I had made progress and wasn't suffering anymore.

Plus, there were plenty of good reasons to not pursue anything else. I had an airtight rationale for settling because of my busy life and the fact that I was tired from managing all the important things I had to do. I was so drained that I had become a shell of my former self and needed to restore my identity. I remember saying I'm tired at least five times a day. It summed up my life story, those two words "I'm tired," and this was the answer to everything. It made perfect sense to rest for a minute.

But how could I rest? I was absolutely and completely miserable at work, and it would not go away. I remember my husband saying, "Well, why don't you figure out what you want and go do it? Take a class or whatever it is you want." I would think, I can't do another damn thing. I'm a mother of two kids. I have this job. What is he talking about? I thought this was what I wanted and what I want isn't the point anyway. I had obligations to fulfill and demands to meet. Before I knew it, I was standing at the door of that same old sacrificing, struggling, suffering trifecta. I was going up or out, but I was not going back to that cycle. I needed something to kick in and force a change.

That was the exact moment and intention level when my father interrupted my complaining to ask, "Who are you?," the biggest question I'd ever been asked, which planted a seed that has been blossoming ever since.

What began as declarations in that excel spreadsheet gave me both possibility and grounding at the same time. Those declarations anchored me in all the goodness of my life with gratitude, appreciation, and vision. I felt clear and restored. I felt whole and worthy. I felt capable and inspired. I thought to myself, I CAN do something I want and I will. I looked at my declarations about what I was good at and passionate about and chose to enroll in a coaching certification program. I stopped settling, and a year later, I became a certified Energy Leadership Coach and started Evók Life by Design, a firm where we design products and programs to transform your life.

By settling, I chose comfort and security over passion and purpose. I had accepted the terms of my settlement without awareness of the total impact. I felt the slow burn of taking what was given versus what I really wanted. I was okay if I felt secure and comfortable in my settling, but when the discomfort became too much, I had to move up or down the scale.

I am grateful my father asked me that one question: "Who are you?" It opened the doorway to move up and toward my purpose. I knew what I wanted without knowing who I was and that was an unsettling reality. Seeing the content of my vision without the context of how I would experience it left me lost. I am grateful I chose to answer the question and that I was moved enough by my definition to become exactly who I imagined.

SHIFTING TO BEING

Dust settles. I don't.
—Author Unknown

Moving out of settling requires a jumpstart. Something to spark intense emotion to get the juices flowing. You can break the routine that comes with settling by reintroducing yourself to just how brilliant, sexy, and badass you are. I'm usually tempted to settle when I think the effort to create what I want is too much or more than I believe I can handle. Once I'm feeling pumped I create accountability to keep me going. It might be a partner, class, or a program. Something to put a stake in the ground for what I want. Settling is very tempting. It's like a rest stop on a long trip, it's necessary to stop, but you don't want to stay there. That said, it's important to know and recognize the anatomy and signs of settling so you don't get stuck and end up sliding down the scale.

Be inspired and passionate. Refueling my feminine energy always moves me out of settling, even if just for a moment. I let in new thoughts and feelings I've never considered and get back in tune with my physical body. Dancing, the ocean, majestic scenery, indulging my senses or expressing myself through conversation or creative pursuits. I close my eyes, breath deep, and write or map out a new idea. I linger in between the minutes. I rest on each beat of my favorite songs. I turn on my Erykah Badu Pandora station and go all in. Oh, and let's not forget the dark chocolate molten lava cake. But that's just me. There's something about immersing myself in what I love that reminds me of how powerful, capable, and divine I am. I give myself permission to luxuriate and get the jolt I need to stop settling and live into the fullness of who I know myself to be. I open myself up to new experiences I've been longing for and wanting but never explored.

Reconnect with your feminine energy, yes even if you are a man. It can be easy to over-subscribe to the logic and forward focus of our masculine energy when work is such a large part of life. Our feminine energy allows us to flow and rediscover passions that fuel creativity. Take account of your skills, talents, and gifts and light the flame of connection between you and your dreams. Create structures that support you at the level of your vision and stay engaged. Be in awe and inspired by your own damn self and become a champion for you.

PART III

DESIGN

Welcome to design! Design is where you move beyond settling and start creating from a clean slate. You have gone through some challenging and sometimes painful experiences of self-discovery where you couldn't distinguish your identity from your circumstances. In design, you have space and clarity and have discovered the truth of who you are separate from what surrounds you. The fog is lifted, and you can see the possibility of what you want being real.

When you move into the design, you open the doors to creativity and start moving toward the powerful energy to reach your goals. You step into a flow where you conceive a vision, align all the elements of your life, your resources, and your time to that vision, and use your creative power to bring it to life.

Chapter 8 | STRIVING

STRIVE NOT TO BE A SUCCESS, BUT RATHER TO BE OF VALUE.

— ALBERT EINSTEIN, THEORETICAL PHYSICIST

EXPERIENCE	ENERGETIC	LEVEL
How you are experiencing the energetic in your life	The energy or signal you're sending out to the universe.	
STRIVING Make great efforts, try hard to achieve. Actively focusing energy to get or obtain something you don't yet possess or have.	**WANTING**	2
	WISHING	1

THE ANATOMY OF STRIVING

2. WHAT THOUGHTS WOULD I THINK?
I WORKED MY WHOLE LIFE FOR THIS, IT'S TIME TO GRIND AND SHINE.

3. WHAT EMOTIONS WOULD I CLAIM?
ENERGIZED, INSPIRED, HOPEFUL.

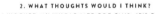

4. WHAT FEELINGS WOULD I EXPERIENCE?
OPENING UP IN YOUR CHEST, LIGHTNESS.

5. WHAT ACTIONS WOULD I TAKE AND NOT TAKE?
CREATE A VISION, STRATEGIZE, MAP OUT A PLAN. EVALUATE AND ANALYZE OPTIONS.

WHAT BELIEFS WOULD I HOLD TRUE?
I CAN DO THIS, I GOT THIS. I DESERVE THIS.

You've made a choice to take the first step in moving toward what you want. Even when you're avoiding or resisting at the lower levels of the intention scale, there is still something you desire. There's always some truth calling your spirit regardless of what level of intention you're experiencing. The key is to be clear about how you are relating to that desire or calling. When you're sabotaging it, you're going to suffer. When you're suppressing or resisting it, you're going to struggle. When you are avoiding or denying it, you're sacrificing. Then when you're indifferent to it, you're settling. When you begin to wish for it and want it, you will strive for it. Striving opens you up to possibility and hope, increasing your connection and desire for your goals. In striving, you become willing to see a vision and give yourself permission to wish and want what you see.

LIVING AND STRIVING

Here's how striving played out for me. I was sitting in an intensive class during my coaching certification program when I received a vision. Clear, bright, and shiny. I saw a beautiful three-story building with windows and an open layout flooded with natural sunlight. I saw people moving freely about from one area to another, engaging in various lifestyle activities from shopping, eating organic delights, and chatting, to working out and participating in workshops on transformation. It felt like walking through heaven for a health and well-being junkie like me. I immediately knew my purpose was to create this space for healing, well-being, and personal revolution.

I was beyond inspired and ready to take whatever action necessary to make this happen. I put all my engineering, project management, product design, and leadership skills to use. I created a strategy, charted a plan, and shared my vision with close family and friends. I felt completely renewed. You wouldn't have recognized me in comparison to a year earlier.

I showed a few close people my plans and was unexpectedly bombarded with perspectives on how risky it would be to take on the overhead of a physical structure. Everyone kept telling me the idea was good, but it would be best to focus on one area, instead of multiple service areas in the same building. Wait, what!? Rewind that—didn't you just hear the divine vision I shared with you? I was scared to even say anything in the first place, and now I'm getting lectured on margins and overhead risk before I even set up my first research date with Google.

Being so inspired and getting lackluster responses to my ideas was deflating. I felt like no one understood my passion—or could match my enthusiasm—and it impacted my confidence. I started to second guess my vision and reigned in the plans to focus on a virtual business reducing some of the risks. Although I had lost some steam, I stayed determined, hustling and on my grind at work, at home, and in my business to keep hope alive. I didn't expect to feel so lonely; I had started out so hopeful. It was a roller coaster ride of high energy and discouraging moments actively trying my hardest to keep the flame from dying out in the face of disbelief. I kept pushing through, but I felt my vision slipping. Each time I got into this space, I recalled my vision. It was clear. A three-story brick-and-mortar building. As crazy as it may sound, that was the vision ... period.

Once I restored the vision, I was back on track and could realign the plan to get things moving again. However, there was no straight path to the promised land. I wasn't sure how to make progress without backtracking or stalling every time I got feedback. I really wanted this dream to work, so I got in-house counsel to weigh in. My husband ran our IT business successfully for almost twenty years, so I knew he could help. The only challenge was his allergy to sugarcoating, and I was already in a vulnerable space. Of course, I got the truth straight, no chaser: "Stop hustling and grinding, doing a whole bunch to feel busy, when you're not moving your business forward."

Bottom line, "You have a project, not a business." I couldn't believe it! This was my God-given vision that he was calling a project. I was hot, but I could not deny what he was saying. I had been running around back and forth, up and down like a chicken with my head cut off. I was working on websites, mapping out plans, and spending hours in meetings that brought in zero revenue.

I was aimlessly striving to make some sort of progress. Each time someone questioned or challenged my idea I took it as a reason to question myself and back off my vision. My striving shifted back and forth from being focused and on purpose to saving my ego from dying the slow painful death of a failed business idea. This disconnect and lack of focus didn't stop me from being busy. I was still on my grind, but without a clear purpose or end goal in sight, my energy was being drained, and my vision was delayed.

The energy of striving is wishing and wanting, which by definition, means you do not have something. You can only wish for and want that which you do not have. Although striving is important to open you up and get you hoping again, staying in the energy of striving will eventually gift an experience of void and lack. If you strive long enough without accomplishing your goal, you can easily dip back into settling, disconnecting from your passion, struggling, or resisting some truth in the way of real progress. Purpose gives meaning to your pursuit and design keeps you in alignment and connected to it. Healthy striving has to have both to keep you moving up the scale and experiencing what you want.

SHIFTING TO BEING

Don't ask yourself what the world needs. Ask yourself what makes you come alive, and go do that, because what the world needs is people who have come alive.

— Harold Thurman, American Author, Civil Rights Leader

Be focused and purposeful. Striving is an intention level full of possibility and activity. It's where productivity and creativity can come alive to manifest your goals. Focused striving is what drives real progress and connecting to purpose is what drives focus. When you are connected to purpose, you have a clear experience and result in mind. Your desired outcomes give light to what matters and give your effort meaning. You know what's relevant and necessary. You also know what's unimportant and can fall away. Without this focus and purpose, striving becomes empty and drains your energy and esteem over time.

I have a thing for striving, it's my default. Remember I'm a doer and there's plenty to do in striving. In my mind, I'm always in pursuit. I'm never there. As a visionary and an innovator, I'm future-focused and striving is the never-ending means to no end. If I'm not careful, I end up all over the place wondering why I'm doing so much and who is getting the benefit. I get exhausted and discouraged if I feel I'm spinning my wheels. I lose patience, and I get frustrated. It takes a constant refocusing to see and feel like I'm moving forward.

Every quarter I BEprint™ I am both deliberate and strategic about redefining my purpose. I design my personal strategy for what the following twelve weeks are going to be all about and define what success looks like to me. The process gets me crystal clear about what I want, what matters to me, what I'll do, and how I'm going to do it. I'm able to identify my personal pathway that has meaning every step of the way and works for me to get the results for which I'm aiming. I'm faithful to the process, and it works to keep me aligned and on target to my goal. Determine what structure works to keep you focused, on purpose, strategic, and deliberate about your life on a regular basis. Like the seasons, everything has its purpose, and significant change can happen even in twelve weeks.

Chapter 9 | SEEKING

WHAT YOU SEEK IS SEEKING YOU

— RUMI, 13TH-CENTURY PERSIAN POET

EXPERIENCE	**ENERGETIC**	**LEVEL**
How you are experiencing the energetic in your life	The energy or signal you're sending out to the universe.	
SEEKING To go in search of, look for, or try to find. Stretching and expanding/ taking on new thoughts, actions, and responses to people or circumstances.	**BELIEVING**	4
	ASKING	3

THE ANATOMY OF SEEKING

2. WHAT THOUGHTS WOULD I THINK?
I'M WILLING TO TRY IT. I'M OPEN TO IT.
WHY NOT?

3. WHAT EMOTIONS WOULD I CLAIM?
MOTIVATED, FOCUSED, CURIOUS, EXCITEMENT,
AND PASSIONATE.

4. WHAT FEELINGS WOULD I EXPERIENCE?
A LITTLE SHAKY, CATCHING AND WATCHING
YOUR BREATH.

5. WHAT ACTIONS WOULD I TAKE AND NOT TAKE?
EXPLORE NEW IDEAS, ENGAGE NEW PEOPLE AND
PLACES. RESEARCH AND GATHER INFORMATION.
PUT PRACTICES IN PLACE TO GROW AND EXPAND.

WHAT BELIEFS WOULD I HOLD TRUE?
THERE'S SOMETHING MORE FOR ME.
EVERYTHING IS POSSIBLE.

Seeking is a deeper more earnest version of striving. It's a humble willingness to accept what you don't know, and still actively engage within yourself, and with others, to find out. Seeking recognizes not only the hopes of what you're wishing for and wanting but also the promise that it can be real. Seeking moves you beyond what is possible based on your personal will alone, and sees the possibilities available with heightened wisdom, trust, belief, and understanding.

This is where you put some skin in the game. Up until this point on the intention scale, much of the work has been an internal exercise centered mostly around your beliefs, thoughts, emotions, and some actions in isolation. When you're at a level of seeking, you start to really engage others in your goals and dreams. Whether it's asking for help in prayer or asking friends for support and accountability, you start to engage the outside world in your pursuit. It's a very vulnerable and authentic experience where you accept the reality of what you don't know and move into uncharted territory that could come with disagreement, disbelief, or rejection. This is a conscious and deliberate faith walk because you have to shed your ego to sincerely expand past your comfort zone.

As a seeker, I am constantly reading something new, and engaging in deep conversations to stretch myself and grow in areas I'm passionate about. I've cultivated a habit of seeking, and it has been one of the biggest blessings I've experienced. During some of the most painful times of my life, I responded with seeking. Something in me was willing to speak my truth and believe in a vision or a solution to my problem I could not see.

Each time I was exposed to something new, I believed I could create and have whatever it was. I remember interviewing for a job in college with the plant manager of a major corporation. I knew very little if anything about a corporate environment, jobs, or titles and what they did. She told me who she was, her role, and what her main responsibilities were. I nodded and said, "Oh, I can do your job." Yes, I said that out loud to her, and yes, she looked at me a little funny. The truth was I had no clue how bold my statement had been. We just moved on with the interview, and by the end of the day, she offered me the job.

My seeker's spirit allowed me to see something, and believe in who I was, and what I could do, or have, even before I had it. I was free enough to see a possibility and verbalize it directly to this woman, without any filter of doubt. Recall, I wasn't familiar with corporate politics at the time, so I wasn't relying on my own knowledge. Something in me believed I could do her job without any tangible evidence.

At the level of seeking, you can consciously create reality because what you believe is literally what you will start to see and experience. Believing is holding a thought as truth. "Seek, and ye shall find." Your body's reticular activation system (RAS) will filter your vision and experience to fit your beliefs. This is your brain's RAS at work. Bringing a thought to the forefront of your mind triggers a hypersensitivity to recognizing it all around you. When you decide you want a black BMW and then you see them all over the place. It's not because hundreds of BMW owners moved near you, it's because your RAS is directing the traffic of what you consciously see according to your primary thought patterns.

On the flipside, seeing may be believing, but believing is still not having. Having requires commitment which we'll get to in the next level. Seeking and believing are necessary steps that move you closer to having. They expand and pull you toward what you want, and transform your vision from a hopeful possibility to a close reality.

Your job is to transform how you operate based on what you see and to boldly act in alignment with it to create it.

SHIFTING TO BEING

I promise if you keep searching for everything beautiful in this world, you will eventually become it.

—Tyler Kent White, Author

Seeking is the beginning of your faith walk. It's less about moving up the scale and out of a specific intention level and more about expanding the experience. Put yourself out there and be willing to stay present and thoughtfully engage with the response you get. When I step out on faith in the spirit of seeking, I get the benefit of actual experience to solidify my truth and remind me the answers are always available.

Be curious and creative, even playful. I usually start seeking when I'm looking for or shifting into something new. I remember shifting my career and trying to figure out who I wanted to be in the world. After fifteen years of being an engineer, I spontaneously chose to introduce myself in a group as a designer for the first time. I was so excited about it. I had found a new way to describe myself that incorporated both my technical and creative sides. The group was completely engaged as I described the product design work I did at the time, I knew I had found the answer. Having a clear and authentic way to express myself was self-affirming and brought me so much joy and freedom.

I have been an engineer, a project manager, a coach, a designer, and now I define myself as visionary and innovator. How do I know? I try each definition on and see how it fits. I see how I'm able to interact and how people respond. The response I get either affirms my definition or gives me some insight I can use to adjust. It's my choice.

Let go of trying to get it right or perfect and take action to get real feedback and find your way forward. If one thing doesn't fit or work, try another. Trust there is something beyond you working on your behalf and remind yourself, your goal is bigger than you. Use your vision to inspire you to take action and move into the experience of what you desire most.

PART IV

LIVE BY DESIGN

Living by design is about taking consistent actions in alignment with your passion, truth, and vision. When you live by design, you own it all: your vision, your goals, your purpose, your intention, all of it. You have a clear vision and walk in integrity with what you see and say regardless of what barriers may arise. Challenges mean nothing here. You are connected to your creative power. You tap into internal and external resources, and you move with purpose and peace towards your goals.

Your grateful attitude from the joyful knowing of who you are, from living what you want, and from experiencing what matters most to you is in the very breath you take.

You are inside the ultimate fulfillment of your passion.

Your purpose is living your calling and truthfully sharing your results!

Chapter 10 | SURRENDERING

*BEFORE THE TRUTH CAN SET YOU FREE, YOU NEED TO
RECOGNIZE WHICH LIE IS HOLDING YOU HOSTAGE*

— RACHEL WOLCHIN, ARTIST.

EXPERIENCE
How you are experiencing the energetic in your life

ENERGETIC
The energy or
signal you're
sending out to
the universe.

LEVEL

SURRENDERING

To cease resistance and relinquish control to a greater power.
Acknowledging and aligning with truth.

KNOWING	6
COMMITTING	5

THE ANATOMY OF SURRENDERING

2. WHAT THOUGHTS WOULD I THINK?

THIS IS GOING TO BE SO GOOD. I'M HERE AND
IT'S TIME.

4. WHAT EMOTIONS WOULD I CLAIM?

RELIEVED, NURTURED, SUPPORTED, GRATEFUL
AND JOYFUL. FREE!

3. WHAT FEELINGS WOULD I EXPERIENCE?

WARM INSIDE. TINGLING SENSATION IN
YOUR BODY. SOFTENING OF YOUR POSTURE,
RELAXING INTO YOUR BODY.
DEEP BREATHING.

5. WHAT ACTIONS WOULD I TAKE AND NOT TAKE?

RELEASE AND SHIFT NEGATIVE ENERGY
TO WORK FOR YOU. RESPOND VS REACT TO
CIRCUMSTANCES. WORK WITH THE
FLOW OF REALITY.

WHAT BELIEFS WOULD I HOLD TRUE?

LIFE IS GOOD. ALL THINGS ARE WORKING FOR ME.
THIS IS BIGGER THAN ME AND BETTER THAN I
COULD IMAGINE.

When you surrender, you open yourself up fully to your goal or calling. You accept and embrace a greater purpose in what you want, and give up controlling the outcome. It's a powerful act of humility, integrity, and trust.

Surrendering means you acknowledge both your true spirit and your ego, your light and dark, strengths and flaws. In other words, you see all sides of your experience and operate from a perspective of wisdom and harmony. You are neither better nor worse than others, and you are not solely focused on self—or indulgent—in your own esteem, be it low or high. In surrendering, you acknowledge not just your truth, but bigger truths about humanity—even the universe—and you let those guide your actions.

Surrendering frees you up and opens the door to real commitment. Up until this point on the intention scale, you've been back and forth, up and down, regarding your dedication to your goal. You've been gaining energy and confidence with each level, but not quite enough to be reliable in your pursuit. When you surrender and allow that force greater than you to work with and through you, big things start to happen. You begin to see how the universe wants to aide you. As it does, you gain a knowing in your spirit and the confidence to be consistent.

Consistently choosing in alignment with your goal, particularly when there's difficulty, is a commitment, and commitment is required to achieve any big result. Whether it's a relationship, building a business, or living a healthy lifestyle, to succeed your actions must match your goals moment to moment and day to day.

Recall my bright, shiny vision of a brick and mortar transformational wellbeing center. In the age of virtual coaching and online classes, I was basically told, "Build it and they will *not* come." At times, I mentally suffered over having such a huge vision with seemingly no way to physically create it. This was such a struggle. I felt like why me? This is crazy! It's too risky! It just doesn't make any *sense*. Where will I get the capital to do something like this? Full-time employment and a steady paycheck had conditioned me well, so I thought the only way to get enough money for the building was to grow the business enough to pay for it. Although this wasn't a bad idea and it had some wisdom to it, it wasn't at all efficient. I spent tons of energy and effort part-time with little cash flow to create traction and momentum. All the while continuing to be miserable and overwhelmed at my day job. I put in crazy hours and built a solid brand and product, but it was a long and slow road with several bumps that were undermining my faith and belief.

I didn't want to shut it all down. I reasoned, what if I had misinterpreted the vision? I thought, maybe the building was a metaphor for how to run the virtual business model. I started to sacrifice the bigger picture and focus on a smaller version of what I thought I could achieve. I settled for an easier and more sensible business model which worked for a while bringing in revenue and new clients. I focused on serving, and the impact was amazing.

People were completely transforming their lives by BEprinting™, and it got harder and harder to deny the voice within me. I was dreaming about my vision and constantly strategizing ways to create it. It was simply impossible to avoid the big vision.

I became re-energized and started to engage others. My seeker self-kicked in, and I started to strive towards clarity. I began to believe again that a physical center could happen. I reconnected to just how much I wanted this building.

As I started asking people how to do this, it still wasn't a straight answer of *yes*. I heard some of the same pushback of too risky and too much overhead. Up and down the scale I went, I had been through this scenario before, but instead of reacting from a fear of failure I took a different route. I let the fear in without denying, avoiding, rationalizing, or fighting it. What if they are right and it is too risky? So what? Risk can be mitigated. What does that mean and how does that impact the plan if I'm committed to this vision because I know it is going to become real? That reframe changed the whole game.

Now I interpreted the pushback, differently, it wasn't pushback, it was a legitimate business challenge that would need a solution and a plan to address it. I stopped defending and proving and started asking questions. I asked questions seeking clarity instead of approval, which also led to me asking new people for different perspectives. What changed the most was me.

I had finally gone through enough on this business journey to recognize who I had become, so I heard people's responses differently. I had stopped seeing people's opinions as threats and began to discern the truth in them, and throw away the rest. I stopped allowing myself to doubt, second guess, or rationalize away the vision. I got with myself and said, "Look, you know the vision you received, it was clear. You're either doing this or not, what's the deal?"

Once I made it plain to myself I had a clear answer: "Let's go!" That was my big surrender moment. I let go, and I breathed deeply. What a damn relief! This is the vision. I don't know exactly how this is going to happen, but I know some things. I know some people, and I now know this energetic experience I'm having that's affirming I have everything I need.

I felt washed over with gratitude. I felt like, all this time I had been suffering, struggling, striving, and all of it was now complete. I was now experiencing this different greater energy soothing me and smoothing out my road.

Taking consistent action, persisting through challenges, and still declaring *yes* to my vision, was a demonstration of commitment that built a knowing in my spirit beyond my own will. I committed to my vision. I let go of the false burden of struggling for the illuminating wholeness of knowing.

Surrendering strengthened my commitment. The release and relief of having a clear vision and knowing there's much more than my ego at work to create this vision built my confidence. When I surrendered, I moved further into alignment with my own spirit and its vision. My big moment of surrender has since become a moment to moment way of being that allows me to operate with greater conviction toward my goals. There are still struggles and challenges but not with the same things over and over again. Life is bigger and better each moment I surrender and let it in.

SHIFTING TO BEING

By surrendering, you create an energy field of receptivity for the solution to appear.
—Dr. Wayne Dyer

Be patient and steadfast. Acknowledge the forces working on your behalf beyond your own will. See how what appears to be a threat or a challenge is actually working for your good. Look for and recognize synchronicities as confirmation and evidence to reinforce beliefs that serve your purpose. Go beyond the believing with your mind to the knowing in your soul that you are enough, you are ready, and what you want is coming to life.

I can get very swept away in my emotions, so I am deliberate about staying objective and optimistic to keep things moving. There are points in the day, and times of the month, where I simply don't have the energy to manage the emotional waves. I've learned a single practice of tapping in instead of tapping out, and I believe many lives have been saved as a result.

Tapping out causes me to blame others or feel powerless. Tapping in allows me to see and feel the truth that everything is alright. There is no threat, things are happening for my highest good, and I am fine. These truths allow me to release the tension and surrender. Surrendering feels like a warm hug. When I'm in the fifty-car-long drive-thru line at Chic-fil-A, and the children are in the backseat arguing after I'm already behind on my errands for the day, I close my eyes and breathe. I tell myself I am perfectly fine in this moment because it is divinely ordered and nothing is going to fall apart, unravel, or come undone if I sit still and be where I am. There are a hundred of these moments a day, some at home, some at work, some with friends, and some when I'm by myself. There is more than enough opportunity to practice so when I find myself *grinding or hustling* for my businesses or the household to the point of frustration, I can surrender.

I see surrendering as getting out of the way of what's trying to help me even if I can't see it or exactly what it's doing. When I'm lagging twenty minutes behind schedule all morning long, it's a signal to slow down, take a few deep breaths, and take something off of the list. When my brain starts replaying the ten things I have to get done, I say to myself, "Who are you and what's the next thing for you to do." I choose one thing and let the others be until it's their turn. I can surrender because I know that the way I'm committed to living, with peace, love, and freedom, is good and full of high intention and high intention always fulfills its purpose. I keep that awareness present in my spirit, and I stay mindful at the moment to honor my commitment. A life left to my frustrations, impatience, or exhaustion is not my commitment. I know my purpose and real commitments, and that's where my energy lives.

Chapter 11 | SOVEREIGNTY

YOU GET THERE BY REALIZING YOU ARE ALREADY THERE.

— ECKHART TOLLE, *BESTSELLING AUTHOR OF THE POWER OF NOW*

EXPERIENCE	ENERGETIC	LEVEL
How you are experiencing the energetic in your life	The energy or signal you're sending out to the universe.	

SOVEREIGNTY

Supreme power or authority to govern yourself. Being present and able to respond with power and confidence in any moment.

EMBODYING 7

THE ANATOMY OF SOVEREIGNTY

2. WHAT THOUGHTS WOULD I THINK?
IT IS DONE. THIS IS WHO I AM, THIS IS WHAT I'M DOING. I'M CLEAR AND PURPOSEFUL ABOUT WHAT I'M CREATING.

3. WHAT EMOTIONS WOULD I CLAIM?
POWERFUL, ASSURED, CONFIDENT, DELIBERATE AND PURPOSEFUL.

4. WHAT FEELINGS WOULD I EXPERIENCE?
EVEN AND STEADY BREATHING. YOU'RE AWARE OF INTERNAL SENSATIONS AND EXTERNAL MOVEMENTS.

5. WHAT ACTIONS WOULD I TAKE AND NOT TAKE?
OBSERVE YOURSELF AND LIFE, CHOOSE YOUR ACTIONS.DELIBERATELY, CELEBRATE!

WHAT BELIEFS WOULD YOU HOLD TRUE?
I AM A CREATOR. I AM CONNECTED WITH MY SOURCE. I AM WHOLE AND COMPLETE. I CAN CREATE AND HAVE WHAT I WILL.

Having sovereignty and embodying means you are it, you are what you've been seeking, you're already there.

You're always embodying some way of being that gives you sovereignty over some part of your life. The question is what is it, and, is it what you want? There is something in your life that is predictable, you keep repeating the habit, experience, or cycle of it. It's happening by design. For example, you embody strength, you're the friend everyone leans on, calls, and comes to in a crisis. You take on tough situations and make shit happen. That's what you do, it's who you are, and it's how people see you.

When circumstances are hard, you dominate and have complete authority in handling your business. That's what sovereignty is like. The key is whether your sovereignty feels like freedom, independence, and autonomy because you're wielding your power on purpose; or if it locks you into being obligated to handle things that don't matter to you and only benefits others.

I've finally developed sovereignty over my time, energy, and peace of mind. I used to be a fragmented, seriously frazzled hot mess—always on edge and snappy. Doing too much. Spending my time and energy on people, places, and things that didn't matter. Resenting everyone for pulling me in different directions. I was in a constant struggle trying to decide what wasn't going to get done and feeling guilty for not being able to do it. I could not win.

I had declared myself an entrepreneur. I had enthusiastically accepted my calling and committed to my vision. I was all in—

except for the part where I was still a full-time employee in a demanding job, with a husband and two children all of whom valued me for the predictability, hard work, and the security I provided.

I had the typical working mother's morning routine; wake up, get the kids up and dressed while trying to get in a quick workout or meditation. Get myself dressed while checking emails, then make breakfast, and handle drop off while taking a conference call or two. Once again, I was all in and had the routine down—minus the constant anxiety, increasing inability to concentrate, and the ready-to-cuss-you-out-at-any-time disposition. I called that time between six and nine in the morning, the pre-shift because it was only the beginning of a pattern that played out for the rest of the day.

The first shift was my day job, the second shift was homework, sports practice, dinner, and the kids' bedtime, and the third shift was couple time which went until around eleven o'clock. Then there was a fourth shift, the night shift, just for me. From about eleven until one in the morning, I could focus and make whatever progress I could on my business vision.

Every day, not counting my five hours of sleep, I spent 90% of my time and energy answering the demands of others. This was my schedule for four years until my body revolted.

In the beginning, I leveraged a work-from-home schedule to counterbalance the load. After a year or so, my flexible work arrangement proved to be a constant battle given the stigma and scrutiny from other leaders in the office. As a result of the constant scrutiny, the work environment became more and more toxic. My family and the little time I had to work on my business became my lifeline.

Another year went by, and I started getting chronically sick. The flu, sinus infections, and fatigue all took turns knocking me out. My doctor was adamant about me changing my work environment for over a year, but in my mind, there was nothing I could do. I focused on exercising regularly, eating healthy, meditation, and prayer. I drank water, I took a vacation, and for three months straight I added a weekly massage, acupuncture, and vitamin C IV flush to my schedule. I called it my Healthy Hour. All that and I was still sick and tired.

My epiphany came when I watched a video a friend sent me called, Why Your Self-Care Regimen Isn't Working. The answer was obvious, and I had still missed it; your self-care regimen isn't working because you won't remove the stressor. Basically, I had unconsciously put myself on life support to survive the toxic and chronic stress of my day job. I knew it was time to let go of it, and even though it was literally draining my health, I reasoned the stability was more important. I finally pulled the plug when I returned to work healthy from the holiday break and didn't make it through the day before I had to go to urgent care. I had the flu, and my doctor pulled me out of work to recover. It was at that point that I listened and I chose to remove the stressor.

The truth is, I always had the authority. It was my time, my energy, and my peace of mind. I was just afraid to use my authority. I became subordinate, and my identity was wrapped up in my day job, my role as a wife and mother, and my attachment to stability and loyalty. There was nothing wrong or bad about me or these parts of my life but the way I related to them, as self-identifying attachments, made them a prison.

My immune system could not take the inner conflict between being a visionary, health activist, and an entrepreneur on one side; and being an employee in a toxic environment trying to *balance* work, home, and business on the other side. I was completely out of alignment, and the only way to recover and restore my health was to use my power over every aspect of the situation, not just the easy parts. I took my doctor's advice and pressed pause on everything. I even agreed to a leave of absence from work.

As divine order would have it, within a couple of weeks, my company announced a separation program and severance package for a segment of the business that included my role. Coincidence? I think not.

When I finally chose to embody my power over my time, energy, and peace, life opened up. I am now a full-time entrepreneur, I work from home or wherever I choose, I take my time in the mornings and focus on one beautiful thing at a time. I focus on wellbeing because it is one of my core values and it feels amazing. Beyond that, I can now enjoy my health practices as a way to proactively care for myself; not to survive a constant stress and threat.

Sovereignty is about consciously embodying a way of being that is aligned with your values, passions, goals, purpose, and your highest vision. This is not always easy. You have a lot of practice at reacting from emotion and feelings instead of responding from purpose and vision. If you can master being authentically present at the moment responding with confident aligned intention, you have sovereignty.

With sovereignty comes true authentic power. You are able to govern yourself and create any outcome you want with grace and authority.

SHIFTING TO BEING

Remind yourself. Nobody built like you, you designed yourself.
—Jay–Z, hip-hop magnate, from "A Dream"

Sovereignty is pure self-governance and unshakeable ownership of your time, energy, and peace of mind. This is where you want to be on the scale, present and embodying a fulfilling, meaningful, and impactful experience of living.

Be enthusiastic about your life and your vision. Be all in for what you know is possible and stand in a clear definition and design of who you are and what you're building. Set a compelling vision, a clear purpose, a daily aim, and anchor yourself with positive intention. Act deliberately and plan your time in alignment with your aim. Always, always appreciate. Live free in the moment, be present, and create the results and experiences you envision.

Be original and authentic, often referring back to the fact that you are star stuff and remembering the core anatomy of your highest level of intention. You are designed to win. You have everything you need to be who you want, create what you want, live how you want ... period. Take that as a friendly reminder. There's no question or doubt about it, but sometimes we forget. It's like going home for the holidays, hearing your mother's voice, and regressing to being a teenager when you're forty-something. You can't help yourself. If you don't consistently remind yourself who you are, you will forget.

I find myself in situations trying to convince or prove something. I sometimes hear the tone of my voice as complaining or explaining and say, Wait ... what? Who is this talking, and why is she tripping like she doesn't know who she is?

It's a moment to moment thing. I redesign who I am on a quarterly basis and design what I do weekly and daily. I am a planner addict. I use daily tools both paper and electronic to keep my focus clear and to stay mindful of who I am and what I'm up to. It grounds me and puts everything in perspective. By doing so, I remind myself of my power and authority to create what I want and live on my terms. This is my sovereignty. This is being satisfied and fulfilled. This is making a difference and owning what matters most to me; my time, my energy, and my peace of mind.

CHAPTER 12

EXPANDING INTENTION

I have come to believe that each of us has a personal calling that's as unique as a fingerprint, that the best way to succeed is to discover what you love, and then find a way to offer it to others in the form of service, working hard, and also allowing the energy of the universe to lead you.

— Oprah Winfrey

Your intention is more than a thought, it's more than a belief, and it's more than what you hope, wish, or want to happen. You don't *have* an intention, you *are* intention. Your intention is the energetic and experiential sum of who you are being at any moment. It sets the tone for you, others, and the universe as a message about who you are and what you're creating in your life.

What you have and how you experience life is a direct result of your intention. It dictates how you vibrate and therefore what scope of results are available to you. Intention is literally the creative source and driving force behind your actions, so it determines what you do, and the level of intensity, focus, and power you have in doing it. Your intense, focused power in action is the fuel for everything you create. Becoming aware of your intensity and consciously directing that power allows you to have authority over who you are, what you do, and what you have.

Over time you and your results will expand, and your impact on others will grow. You will build the muscle and ability to move up the scale a level or two at a time. It takes patience, focus, and willingness. There will be times when you dip, and it's not a bad thing because there can be something useful and purposeful to be gained from all of it. When you suffer, you can shed old ways and purify your spirit. When you struggle you can strengthen your resolve, and mindful sacrifices can create space and support tremendous accomplishments. When you are conscious of your intention, you can employ it to create unimaginable results. The more you practice the framework of the BEprint™ Intention Scale and deliberately move from level to level, the more muscle you build at owning your energy.

That's really the goal, to free yourself up from aimless suffering and struggling and to expand and experience sovereignty that allows you to fully express yourself, impact others, and to fulfill and be fulfilled in your purpose.

This method is not a cure-all solution to life's problems. This is a process and a tool for you to become a master of your ego self and tap into your higher self. I wrote this book to distinguish concepts we often confuse and collapse and to offer language that provides clarity and frees you up.

I want you to embrace how much good there is in life, and to receive pleasure from it more than you suffer, struggle, sacrifice, settle, or even strive. I want you to seek and see your purpose and truth and experience the immense joy and gratitude of surrendering. I ask you to be willing to move up the scale and embrace the fulfilling power of sovereignty to positively impact others.

As a human being, this is your power. No matter what life throws at you, you will have the choice and the tools to own your intention and create what you want at will.

Love and Light!

CHAPTER 13

IT'S YOUR TURN

Design is a plan for arranging elements to accomplish a particular purpose.
—Charles Eames, American Designer

On the remaining pages, I ask you to answer the question: *Who are you?* You get to define who you are, design your anatomy, and write your own story. To start you'll find a simple structure to help you create the picture. You can choose one specific area of focus such as health, career, creativity, etc. or you can think about your life overall. Start by declaring an I AM statement that evokes the highest inspiration and intention in that area or for your life. Then design an anatomy that aligns with your I Am declaration by defining each individual element starting with your core beliefs. If you were already this being, what would you have to believe about yourself, others, and the world in general to fully embody the I AM statement? Next, write your own personal mantra, what thoughts would you think regularly? What feelings in your body would you experience and how would you interpret them as emotions? For example, would you feel your heart beating fast and interpret it as the emotion of excitement or anxiety? You get to choose. What actions would you consistently take and what actions would you stop taking?

Don't forget your standards and boundaries. What do you require, what's simply a preference, and what is unacceptable? Now that you're grounded in who you are, expand on your definition. Use the blank note pages to write or rewrite your own story. Write about what you truly desire? What matters to you most and what you envision for yourself? Who's on your support team and what's your personal theme song? Include every detail necessary to get clear and convicted to create your design in real life. Then choose. Choose one action you can take right now to embody your personal design and repeat. Center yourself around who you are and then choose the next action that aligns and evokes your highest intention and experience in this life. This is the practice of owning your energy, time, and your precious peace of mind.

Much love and many, many blessings. Thank you!
Radiah

WHO ARE YOU?

It all begins with this one question. Use the illustration below to define and design the anatomy of being you envision yourself embodying. Start with your *I AM* statement as a declaration of who you would be as the highest version of YOU. Don't over think it. Clear your mind, take a deep breath, and declare what speaks to your heart.

I AM _____

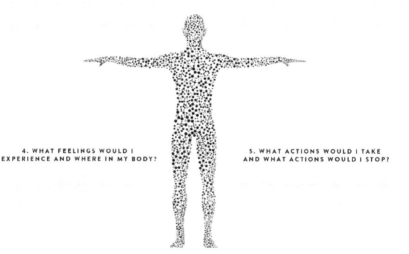

2. WHAT THOUGHTS WOULD I THINK? WHAT'S MY PERSONAL MANTRA?

3. WHAT EMOTIONS WOULD I CLAIM?

4. WHAT FEELINGS WOULD I EXPERIENCE AND WHERE IN MY BODY?

5. WHAT ACTIONS WOULD I TAKE AND WHAT ACTIONS WOULD I STOP?

1. WHAT DO I BELIEVE ABOUT ME, OTHERS, OR THE WORLD IN GENERAL?

STANDARDS + BOUNDARIES — What behaviors from myself or others are...

REQUIREMENTS   **PREFERENCES**   **UNACCEPTABLE**

BEING
IS THE
NEW DOING

_____

_____

_____

_____

_____

_____

_____

_____

_____

_____

BEING
IS THE
NEW DOING

_____

_____

_____

_____

_____

_____

_____

_____

_____

_____

BEING
IS THE
NEW DOING

_____

_____

_____

_____

_____

_____

_____

_____

_____

_____

BEING
IS THE
NEW DOING

_____

_____

_____

_____

_____

_____

_____

_____

_____

_____

BEING
IS THE
NEW DOING

_____

_____

_____

_____

_____

_____

_____

_____

_____

_____

BEING
IS THE
NEW DOING

_____

_____

_____

_____

_____

_____

_____

_____

_____

_____

BEING
IS THE
NEW DOING

_____

_____

_____

_____

_____

_____

_____

_____

_____

_____

BEING
IS THE
NEW DOING

BEING
IS THE
NEW DOING

_____

_____

_____

_____

_____

_____

_____

_____

_____

_____

BEING
IS THE
NEW DOING

_____

_____

_____

_____

_____

_____

_____

_____

_____

_____

_____

BEING
IS THE
NEW DOING

_____

_____

_____

_____

_____

_____

_____

_____

_____

_____

BEING
IS THE
NEW DOING

_____

_____

_____

_____

_____

_____

_____

_____

_____

_____

BEING
IS THE
NEW DOING

BEING
IS THE
NEW DOING

_____

_____

_____

_____

_____

_____

_____

_____

_____

_____

BEING
IS THE
NEW DOING

BEING
IS THE
NEW DOING

BEING
IS THE
NEW DOING

BEING
IS THE
NEW DOING

BEING
IS THE
NEW DOING

BEING
IS THE
NEW DOING

_____

_____

_____

_____

_____

_____

_____

_____

_____

_____

BEING
IS THE
NEW DOING

_____

_____

_____

_____

_____

_____

_____

_____

_____

_____

BEING
IS THE
NEW DOING

_____

_____

_____

_____

_____

_____

_____

_____

_____

_____

BEING
IS THE
NEW DOING

_____

_____

_____

_____

_____

_____

_____

_____

_____

BEING
IS THE
NEW DOING

_____

_____

_____

_____

_____

_____

_____

_____

_____

_____

BEING
IS THE
NEW DOING

BEING
IS THE
NEW DOING

_____

_____

_____

_____

_____

_____

_____

_____

_____

_____

BEING
IS THE
NEW DOING

_____

_____

_____

_____

_____

_____

_____

_____

_____

_____

BEING
IS THE
NEW DOING

_____

_____

_____

_____

_____

_____

_____

_____

_____

_____

BEING
IS THE
NEW DOING

BEING
IS THE
NEW DOING

_____

_____

_____

_____

_____

_____

_____

_____

_____

_____

_____

Author Radiah Rhodes is passionate about engineering dreams into reality. As a well-being innovator, an energy practitioner, and a twenty year veteran of Fortune 100 corporate America, she has mastered both the art of transformative thinking and the science of converting concepts into tangible, proven results.

www.evoklife.com

www.radiahrhodes.com